THEM DAYS

From the Memories of Joan Bellan

by

JOY LAKEMAN

TABB HOUSE

First published in 1982
Tabb House, 11 Church Street, Padstow, Cornwall, PL28 8BG
Reprinted 1987

Printed in Great Britain by
Penwell Ltd., Parkwood,
Callington, Cornwall.

© *Joy Lakeman*
Drawings © *Robin Armstrong*

ISBN 0 907018 15 7

Dedication
To Joan and Geoff for their love and encouragement.

The author thanks Robin Armstrong for providing the chapter heading drawings, Joan Bellan, George Phillips, Margaret Rogers, Nigel Rolstone, and Jim Thorington for permission to reproduce photographs, and Plymouth City Library for access to old newspaper files and for use of its micro-film viewer.

This book is based on one person's recollections. The author has done her best to check details where possible and apologises for any inaccuracies that may have gone unnoticed.

Jacket cover: Joan (on right) aged 7, with sisters Barbara, 6, Hilda, 9, and brother Alf, 2.

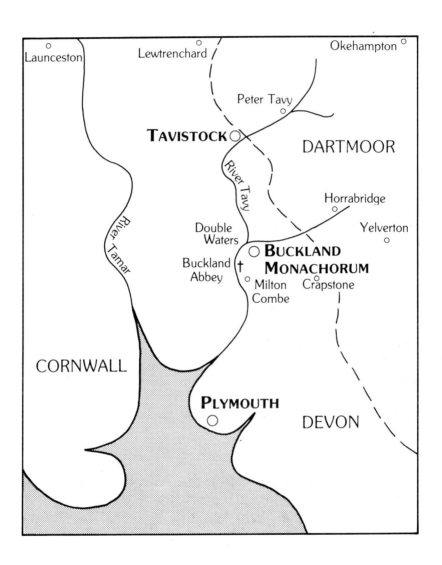

Launceston
Lewtrenchard
Okehampton

Peter Tavy

TAVISTOCK

DARTMOOR

River Tavy

Horrabridge

Double
Waters

Yelverton

River Tamar

Buckland
Abbey

○ **BUCKLAND
MONACHORUM**

Milton
Combe

Crapstone

CORNWALL

PLYMOUTH

DEVON

CONTENTS

Page

List of Illustrations   v

Introduction   vii

Chapter One
Footman and Nursemaid: Joan's Servant Parents   1
The Ghosts of Lew Trenchard   5
Tavistock Coaching Days, the Peter Tavy Tragedy
and the Move to Horrabridge   8

Chapter Two
The Move to Buckland   16
"Saturday Night was Bath Night"   22
"Washday was Monday"   24
The Clothes they Wore   26
Children's Chores   29

Chapter Three
In the Kitchen   33
Recipes   38
Wine-Making   40

Chapter Four
Charmers, Pixies and Superstitions   42
Remedies   47
Infant Mortality   51

Chapter Five
"The Games we Played"   54
Leisure Time   58
Feasts and Festivals   62

Chapter Six
Church and the Squarson   68
Sunday School and Excursions   73

Chapter Seven
Shops and Characters   77
The Terrible Shootings   87

Chapter Eight
"Nearest to School and Latest to Get There"   90
The Great War   95
In Service   97

Chapter Nine
Then . . . and . . . Now   105

Notes and Bibliography   111

LIST OF ILLUSTRATIONS

Page

1   Lew Trenchard House.   3
2   Tom Kelloway driving for Backwell's around the turn of   9
    the century, outside what is now the Burrator Inn, at
    Dousland, for a wedding.
3   The River Tavy, during summer.   11
4   Joan, aged about four, astride a fine dapple grey, with   14
    her father, mother, and sisters, while Tom Kelloway was
    coachman for the Collier family at Foxham's.
5   Paul Bellan, an acknowledged gardener, with his first-   17
    prize parsnips at a West Devon show. He is also
    renowned for his onions weighing several pounds and
    giant potatoes, carrots, and other vegetables.
6   A view of Buckland Monachorum showing one of the old   31
    cottages that has since disappeared.
7   Another view down Buckland main street, in about 1940.   36
8   A studio portrait of Joan taken in Plymouth about 1920.   44
9   Joan and Paul Bellan on their Golden Wedding day,   50
    14th August, 1979, at Rose Cottage.
10 The Manor Inn, as it was in 1919. Mrs Margaret Rogers,   61
    who kindly provided the photograph, is the girl nearest
    the pub door. The tall boy could be Alf Bellan. The
    notice on the wall above the children is a recruiting
    poster for the Royal Navy.
11 St Andrew's Church, which stands near Rose Cottage,   70
    today.
12 Charabanc outings were a big treat, and this hard-   75
    wheeled, open-topped monster was considered a
    luxurious form of transport. The picture shows a
    Buckland Baptist Chapel annual outing.
13 No. 1, The Village, the scene of the terrible murder and   88
    suicide, as it looks today.

14   'Hellfire Jack' was the nickname the villagers gave to   104
     Paul when he bought the first motor-cycle in the village.
     Joan says: "All the girls thought he was smashing and
     kids used to ask for rides."
15   Red Cross nurses form a guard of honour outside the   106
     south door of Buckland church for Joan and Paul's
     wedding on 14th August, 1929. As a young woman,
     Joan was a member of the Voluntary Nursing Service.
16   Rose Cottage today lives up to its name, with red roses   110
     climbing up the front. The author's home, formerly the
     village shop, is next door. Both buildings are listed as
     being of historic and architectural interest, and are
     among the oldest in Buckland Monachorum.
17   Buckland's ancient pub, the Drake Manor. The brook,   110
     which was for years the village's only water supply, runs
     under the road by the nearest car.

INTRODUCTION

FROM THE HOUSE I now live in, with a hillside view over Buckland Monachorum, I can see the roof of the cottage that was my home for four years. It was there that I first had the idea for *Them Days*. I often sat gazing through leaded windows, and felt privileged to watch a scene that had changed little for centuries. The row of white-painted cottages opposite lay in the shadow of the solid, grey walls of the 15th century St Andrew's Church. I could see the crude granite mounting stone, or 'upping' block, common to many West Country villages, which riders still use.

Horses frequently clip-clop past our old front door, although most of the traffic today consists of cars and buses, and with the advent of new building in the village there is a constant stream of bone-shaking heavy lorries.

It is curious that the rumble and buzz of motors passes virtually unnoticed, but at the first hint of an approaching horse, adults and children rush to the windows. Seventy years ago the horse was commonplace and the stampede to the windows would have been to witness the arrival of an early motor car.

Smoke rises from a rooftop jumble of soot-stained chimney pots, for even in these days of central heating many village folk prefer to see and feel a warming open fire. On chill winter days the main street of Buckland is full of a nostril-tingling mixture of coal and wood smoke.

Tucked in behind this little cluster of houses is the village post office and general store, where a liberal amount of local gossip is exchanged with every purchase. Directly opposite and at times seemingly bursting at the seams is the local inn, the Drake Manor. It was built originally as a church house and used since as a maltings and hostelry, and has welcomed travellers since Drake's day.

It is a lucky stranger who chances upon this hideaway village, for as the 21st century approaches, more and more people look, not to the future, but to the past, yearning to live like their old country

vii

cousins. Urban dwellers, some of them city born and bred, now seek refuge in the countryside, and cottages are snapped up as soon as they appear in the estate agents' windows. Families are rushing to adopt the village way of life, to immerse themselves in the community spirit that is unique to rural living.

Far from being forgotten, the age-old skills of making butter, cheese and cream, are being avidly copied. Every square-foot of soil is devoted to vegetables, and back gardens, including my own, are a clutter of clucking hens. Goats nibble the hedgerows. Self-sufficiency is all the rage.

Many of us are fascinated by the way our forefathers survived in ages without the conveniences of modern transport, education electricity, television, radio, medicine, running water . . . not to mention the silicon chip. So I was delighted on moving into a charming centuries-old cottage of my own to discover a walking encyclopaedia of village knowledge on my doorstep, my next-door neighbour. She and her husband, Joan and Paul Bellan, occupy the same neat, whitewashed low-beamed cottage that was her childhood home, whose sturdy cob walls are cool in summer and warm in winter.

From the first cup of tea I drank in Joan's spotless little kitchen I realised that here was someone who could provide a unique insight into life in this area over the past seventy years. Many elderly people like to tell a yarn or two about bygone days, but Joan was exceptional. Her memory was as clear as the sparkling brook which bubbles through the village less than a hundred yards from her door and which, incidentally, was for countless decades the only source of water for the villagers.

"You don't want to hear my old nonsense", was Joan's first modest retort when I ventured to ask if she would mind sharing her memories, but during long hours of conversation I found her to be a fascinating fund of information. I squeezed our talks in between changing nappies, washing dishes, cooking, other household chores, answering the phone, music-making, painting, and a host of other tasks. I make no apology for this not being a scholarly or academic work because I purposely avoided a complicated mass of facts and figures. My intention, in recording Joan's memories, was to let readers eavesdrop on the reminiscences of a Devon housewife. Having accepted the idea of sharing her memories, when nostalgic bits came to mind Joan would come tapping at the back door, anxious to pour out the details. She displayed a fierce pride for the way in which her family humbly but doggedly survived the hard times. Everything was borne with dignity, and the country motto seems to have been 'never complain'.

Here are those fireside memories. Through Joan, young readers may learn for the first time just what life was like in 'them days'. She tells how the horse and carriage ruled the road; of the forelock-tugging era when everybody knew their place and strict class structures still existed; of demanding years 'in service' at the big houses; the rigours of primitive schooling and of deadly days when now commonplace ailments like the 'flu were killers.

You can almost smell the lush, golden loaves as Joan describes with mouth-watering relish how her grandmother baked, using faggots and a cloam oven. This is what I have tried to recapture . . . the minute, homely details of everyday life among ordinary country people, the heartaches and tragedies, simple pleasures, kitchen hints, remedies, and superstitions . . .

I felt compelled to write down Joan's memories for the sake of our grandchildren. And who knows? In decades to come when every chore is carried out by a robot and controlled by a computer, Joan's 'old nonsense' may provide social historians with food for thought. And I bet they'll wish they could have tasted Granny Kelloway's cloam oven bread!

Joy Lakeman. 1982

'The changes that were made since then can easily be seen . . .'

THIS LINE from the song quoted at the beginning of Chapter One rings true in 1987, five years after the first edition of *Them Days* was published.

Sadly, one of those changes has been the loss of my dear friend Joan Bellan whose colourful and evocative memories inspired this book. She was still proudly signing copies of *Them Days* from her sick bed before she died in hospital aged eighty on February 8th 1984.

At her funeral the village church, in whose shadow she had lived for much of her life, was packed in tribute to a much-loved local lady. As I sat with spears of sunlight glinting through the stained glass windows I couldn't help thinking how much she would have enjoyed the occasion.

She lies buried in the nearby graveyard, only a few yards and a stout Devon laurel hedge separating her from her beloved Rose Cottage. With her is her devoted husband Paul who was a sad and lonely man without her and who died on August 26th 1985.

Their joint headstone includes the simple tribute: 'In loving memory of Joan Bellan of Them Days . . .'

Newcomers now occupy Joan's old home but red roses still grow in the tiny front garden of Rose Cottage. Elsewhere in the village changes can indeed be seen. In the four years since this book was written we have welcomed a new vicar, headmaster, shopkeeper, and publican.

New houses have sprung up, bringing with them young villagers whose numbers have necessitated the building of an extension to the already thriving school.

The future of ancient Buckland Monachorum seems assured.

Its past and the lives of today's villagers are all the richer for the memories of *Them Days* which Joan poured out to me and which I am now glad to share with new readers.

Joy Lakeman
1986

CHAPTER ONE

FOOTMAN AND NURSEMAID
JOAN'S SERVANT PARENTS

When I was born some time ago Victoria was queen,
The changes that were made since then can easily be seen,
But I am one of the olden days and maybe thought too slow,
And it's 'give to me the good old days of fifty years ago'.

1

The farmers' sons went out to stock as soon as they could walk,
But now they go to grammar school to teach them how to talk,
They didn't mind the work those days but what a difference now,
They need a machine to milk the cow and a tractor before they
can plough.

The farmer's wife was useful then, her life was never dull,
She never wore silk stockings then but knit her own from wool,
Now home-made bread and home-made cheese are scarcely ever
seen,
And it's 'now you boys must wait for tea 'cos the baker hasn't
been'.

For I am one of the olden days and maybe thought too slow,
and it's 'give to me the good old days of fifty years ago'.

Song: 'Fifty Years Ago.'[1]

IT WAS THROUGH the interest my husband and I have in folk
music that I first shared in Joan Bellan's memories of fifty years
ago and more.

On a bookshelf next to me is a much-coveted copy of *Songs of the
West*, the volume of folksongs from Devon and Cornwall collected
by the celebrated folklorist, writer and squarson, the Rev. Sabine
Baring-Gould M.A. who lived from 1834 to 1924. While I was
thumbing or humming through the book one day soon after moving
into our cottage Joan Bellan, who was with me, asked casually, 'Did
you know my parents met when they were in service with Baring-
Gould?'

That was enough to trigger off my interest and soon Joan
launched into a family history. Joan was born in 1903, but although
she just missed the great Victorian era her early lifestyle was no
different to that of her mother and her grandmother before her.
Joan started her tale at Lew Trenchard House, which is between
Okehampton and Launceston, on the river Lew and just off the
main A.30 road:

That was the home of Reverend Baring-Gould. My
parents met when they were in service there in about
1898. My father, Tom Kelloway, was the footman and he

2

Lew Trenchard House

waited on table as well as looking after the carriage.

It was such a grand family, they had a butler, a footman, a coachman, cooks, maids, nursemaids, the lot. My dad used to generally help out as a servant, like the footmen still do in the royal household nowadays.

My mother was nurse to the two youngest Baring-Gould children who were called Grace and John. They had fifteen children in all, can you believe it? Mam used to tell me all sorts of tales about the family, like how she had to take these two youngest to church every Sunday morning. The little boy, John, was very naughty and he would jump in all the puddles on purpose, although he was supposed to be taken to church looking immaculate. He was always taken out of the house looking smart enough and the church was only across the road but he'd get himself as muddy as he could and she'd have to take him back and let Miss Grace go on with somebody else. Then perhaps one of the older ones, especially one called Julian, put syrup on the door handles for her to catch her glove on. Of course, they had to dress up proper in them days. Mam must have been with the Baring-Goulds for about five years until she got married. 'Twas her only place of service and they were a lovely family to work for.

Everything Reverend Baring-Gould did was marvellous, all the books and things . . . and the hymns. He was the local squire as well, you see. I mean, those sort of people were the only ones who had any money in those days weren't they? Well, he had all those children to bring up . . .

Baring-Gould's best-known hymn was 'Onward Christian Soldiers', written not in Devon as many think but while he was a young curate in Yorkshire. Other hymns from his pen included 'Through the night of doubt and sorrow', 'On the Resurrection morning', and 'Now the day is over'. Joan continued:

4

The reverend used to collect the folk songs too, you know, all the old songs that were dying out. He used to go all over the place to seek them out from the old country folk that were dying. He didn't want the songs to die with them. I think he used to sing them at home as well with the family. He wrote them down together with the music, the whole thing he did ... I don't know how people like him did so much in a day, do you ... ?

Since talking to Joan, I have stumbled across one clue which may answer this question. Baring-Gould's impressive output of writings was probably due to his unusual writing habits which included standing at a lectern late at night and often continuing until the early hours of the morning by the dim flicker of candlelight.

THE GHOSTS OF LEW TRENCHARD

BARING-GOULD'S HOME is still a grand house, which was kept until recently by his descendants as an hotel and restaurant. It is now, however, a private dwelling again. Like many a majestic country manor it boasts its own ghosts. Joan explained:

Oh, yes it's definitely haunted and I remember the tales my Mam used to tell me. There were different stories but one ghost is said to be a bride who is seen all in white running up the driveway. People say either she had an accident going to church or her lover died the night before the wedding was supposed to take place.

Also people have seen someone called 'Madam' in the house, a much older woman. Housemaids have been afraid to stay alone because of Madam walking along the top hall, although Mam told me she was supposed to be very kind. There is a long, long landing on the first floor which is said to be haunted. Mam told me she was an ancestor of the family. She never saw the ghost but knew other members of the staff who did. She heard

5

others tell of the rustle of the old lady's dress and they
were really frightened by it . . .

'Old Madam' was Margaret Belfield Gould, 1711-1795. The tale
goes that she took over the estate when it was in a very dilapidated
condition and spent a weary life putting it in order. So much so, that
she is said to still haunt the wood-panelled long gallery on the first
floor (the landing referred to by Joan) to keep watch over her beloved house. Her portrait hangs, together with many others of the
family, in the dining room.

Next to it is a painting of the other ghost, the younger woman
who was Susanah Gould. She married Peter Truscott, son of the
local rector, despite both families opposing the match. After the
wedding on 19th March, 1729, the bride, who was still in her wedding gown, fell dead in the drive from a heart complaint. She is
known as the 'White Lady' ghost.

The sorry tale of the White Lady is not the only romantic in-
trigue to have emerged from the historic Lew Trenchard House. The
famous vicar sparked off something of a scandal himself with his
choice of wife. According to Joan:

He fell in love with a young, uneducated mill girl
from Yorkshire. She was only sixteen and he sent her
away to be educated and 'finished' with a relative or
friend of his. They were married when she was just eighteen and he was thirty-one and by the time she was 21
she had three children by him.

No member of either family was present at the wedding
ceremony. Mrs Baring-Gould's parents were poor and she herself
was considered illiterate . . . the storm of opposition and gossip that
their wooing must have aroused can be guessed . . .[2]

Joan takes up the story of a happier match, that of her own
parents.

They were there together in service for about two
years and were married at Peter Tavy church by
Reverend Baring-Gould. They went to that village
church because my mother's parents kept the Peter

6

Tavy Inn and my father's family had a smallholding at a place called Lophill about two miles up the road from Lew Trenchard.

The mention of the Peter Tavy Inn was a coincidence for me as it had become a favourite haunt of my husband and myself since we moved to Devon. Baring-Gould himself would be heartened to learn that folk musicians from all over Devon, and even further afield, regularly gather for an impromptu evening of songs and tunes at this meeting place on the edge of Dartmoor. Joan was interested to hear that the lovely old pub is still run on much the same lines as in her grandmother's day. There is a selection of traditional real ales, the original flagstone floors have been kept and crackling log fires welcome the customers in winter. The pub was also the centre of a family tragedy; but to return to Joan:

The Baring-Goulds were very good to their servants, even after they left the house. We always had a goose at Christmas from them when I was young and I had to walk to Yelverton station from Buckland to fetch it. I well remember the last year we had a Christmas gift from them. It was a hare and none of us liked it! It was the sight of it, I think. Mind you, Mrs Baring-Gould had died and the Reverend was an invalid. Anyhow, we weren't left out, this hare was sent, but we'd always had a goose . . .

My mother came out of service when they got married but she used to go back to Lew Trenchard to do the sewing. There's a little crib up in the long gallery and we three (Joan and her two sisters) have all slept in that crib. It's a pretty little wooden one.*

I can remember calling into Lew Trenchard and seeing Baring-Gould on the way to our gran's inn. He was a real aristocrat, not a big man in size, but he still

* This crib is now part of a National Trust exhibition at Killerton House near Exeter.

had the airs of a real gentleman. We used to speak to him but I think we always stood in awe of people like him, more than they do now . . . children'll talk to anybody now in a different way won't they?

His wife I can just remember sitting, sewing . . . a quiet sort of lady, very nice looking.

Joan has been back to Lew Trenchard in recent years and was surprised to find that the room where Baring-Gould died had been turned into a bar.

He died in that room because towards the end he was very ill and had to be downstairs you see.

On my first visit to Lew Trenchard it was an eerie feeling to sit sipping sherry on the deathbed spot of the man who wrote some of our most cherished hymns. I'm sure any late-night reveller, tempted to burst into more ribald song, would find this information a sobering thought!

Baring-Gould thought the world of my mam and she had photos right round our bedroom of everyone in their family. We knew them all by name . . . we'd always known them in the family. Before Mam worked there I think my gran used to go and do the sewing.

Among Joan's treasures is part of a pretty patterned tea-set given to her mother as a wedding present by Baring-Gould. It is still given pride of place in her front room corner cupboard.

TAVISTOCK COACHING DAYS, THE PETER TAVY TRAGEDY AND THE MOVE TO HORRABRDGE

WHEN THEY GOT MARRIED my parents lived in Tavistock in Dolvin Road. It was in flats although they just called them rooms in them days and they lived in

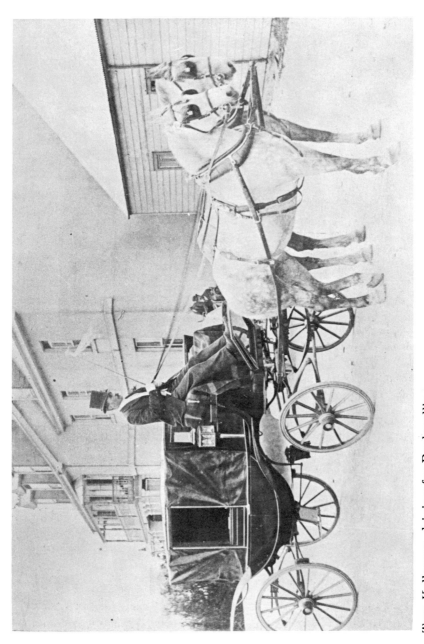

Tom Kelloway, driving for Backwell's

the middle rooms of the house. I didn't know it as a small child because I was too young but after we left there my father's sister took it on and we used to visit. There was a kitchen, a living room and bedroom ... and they had the three of us there.

My father was a coachman on one of those Hackney cabs they had in those days. It was Backwell's he drove for ...

The family firm of S. Backwell still offers a transport service today. It boasts an air-conditioned coach and fleet of daimlers. Stuart Backwell is sad that he has no children to carry on the business and the family name.

"I'm the last of the line; four generations have run the business since 1820. Back in the old days it was really busy, even around Tom Kelloway's time. We catered for the coaching trade; and the pub now known as the Cornish Arms was called the Backwell Arms because the family used to run it. It was quite a concern. You think market day is busy now ... we kept a fiddler playing all day, a baron of beef on the table and we even made our own gin."

The new job Joan's father secured with Backwell's — obviously an improvement on his footman days at Lew Trenchard — was marred by a family tragedy.

My parents had gone to nurse my gran who was ill at the Peter Tavy Inn, and my grandad had to go into Tavistock to get medicine for her. The doctor had been, but you always had to go back to the surgery for the medicine, whatever the weather. Anyhow, on his way back (a tiring round trip of seven miles or more) it was slippery and he must have fallen and rolled into the Tavy. It was March and the weather was cold. If he hadn't hit his head he would have been all right but it killed him 'cos he was found next morning in the river. So my mam and dad had to stay and look after my gran at the Inn ... they went in March and were still there when my sister Hilda was born on June 26th, 1901. Soon afterwards

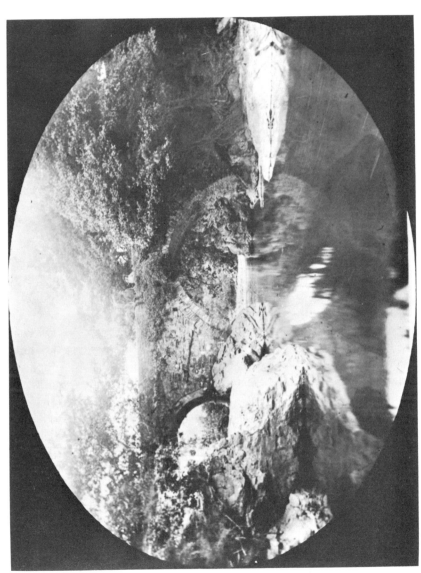

The River Tavy, during summer

they went back to Tavistock where I was born in 1903 and Barbara in 1905.

As modern-day jet fighters scream low over the village on Dartmoor military exercises, it's worth noting that Joan was born in the year of the first flight of a controlled heavier-than-air machine, by Orville and Wilbur Wright.

Then we moved to a big house at Horrabridge called Foxhams with a family called the Colliers. We lived in a lovely big cottage, it's still there with a wing built on. It was a nice white, three-bedroomed house. In those days you had to go down steps to get to it and it was built specially for the coachman. It had the harness rooms and stables all round. I remember there was a big working kitchen and a sort of wash house or back kitchen, and a very large living room. If you look at it from the top of Horrabridge Hill you can look right out over and see the cottage now, and the tree in the garden we used to swing on . . .

Foxhams was owned by Lt Col John Collier. It had been built between 1872-74, and was destroyed by a bad fire in 1956. A modern bungalow now stands on the original foundations in the grounds. In Mrs Bellan's day it had five acres of gardens and four acres of wood and plantations. It was considered very modern since it had a system of electric bells, and well-to-do friends used to visit and inspect the new-fangled contraption with a view to having it installed in their own grand homes.[3]

In the old days some of these woman employers were tartars and Mrs Collier was no exception. She was awful to my father at times. Once, I heard him tell, she locked him in the harness room and she was going to leather him with a horse whip for something he'd done and which she was upset about. Perhaps he'd been drinking or something. There was a pub on Huckworthy Hill and my dad used to pop in there regularly. He used to say his horse always stopped outside, whether he intended going in or not. Perhaps the horse gave the game away one day when the mistress was along. Anyway, he took the whip away from her . . . He had two grooms under him there and I still remember one of them well who said he was going to come back and marry one of us. He was called Edwin Dawe.

But oh, Mrs Collier was a terrible woman at times, specially to the maids in the house. They were always leaving her, usually on Sunday mornings. That's because she was a Catholic and Dad would have to drive her into Plymouth to go to church. Often, when she got home, all the maids had left. Mind you, my Mam said Mrs Collier was always very kind to her. As children we had to be taken up to see her on Sunday mornings at the big house, all dressed up for the occasion. She had very long hair down to her waist, long and flowing it was, and we always seemed to be playing hide and seek in it.

I was about three and a half when we moved to Horrabridge and I first went to school there. Even at three we used to go all day you know, and I can still recall the long, long walk coming and going. There was a boy called Chubb that lived further up the lane and he used to hold our hands and take us. We were given pasties or sandwiches for our lunch . . . the school is where I was first taught to knit, but the girl next to me could always knit much better and faster. I'd let her have mine to knit a bit, then do hers, but I'd only get through a stitch or two for her, while she'd do quite an inch or so for me.

One of Joan's earliest memories of the coachman's cottage is the day when there was a strange noise and a hole suddenly appeared in the ground. In Lt Col Collier's own words: 'A curious thing happened one day when we were all at Plymouth races. It had been a

Joan astride, at Foxham's

very wet summer and when we returned home the coachman's wife (*Joan's mother*) said there had been a strange rumbling at the back of the harness room. We looked, and found a huge pit a few feet away from the harness room had fallen in. It had apparently been the main shaft of an old mine going down 300 - 400 feet.' [3]

Lt Col Collier also described the stabling facilities looked after by Joan's father at Foxhams. 'The stables were a little way away built in a hollow square with a coachman's cottage facing south . . . When I first knew it, it had stabling for three carriage horses, three hunters and three ponies. Used for station work in trap or cart, these were the ponies the children used to ride.'

Joan recalls being allowed to ride these ponies on occasions and also remembers her father having use of the wagonette to drive his family to the Peter Tavy Inn to see Grandma. This same wagonette was used by the Collier family for their picnics at 'beaches' on the Walkham river. Lt Col Collier wrote 'The picnic wagonette had been sent on before with food and drink with the coachman (*Joan's father*), stable boy and parlour maid in charge.'

CHAPTER TWO

THE MOVE TO BUCKLAND

ROSE COTTAGE is the materialisation of every city-dweller's dream. Roses do indeed climb the white-washed walls, walls which have stood for nearly 500 years. Together with the author's home, Rose Cottage is one of the oldest dwellings in the village centre, and both are protected buildings. The little front garden is a splash of colour long before, and after, everyone else's blooms. In the back garden, Paul Bellan nurtures onions, carrots, swedes and other vegetables, of gargantuan proportions, which annually sweep the board at local horticultural shows.

This is the home Joan has known for seven decades, although during their married life the Bellans have lived elsewhere in the Parish of Buckland.

We moved in here when I was seven and a half, because my father had taken a different job as a coachman

Paul Bellan with a first prize

with the Lopes family in Maristow. He was a true horseman and people often brought their young horses to be schooled by him. I can see him now outside the cottage on the back of these mad, wild horses which he broke in, their feet kicking right up on the Baptist Chapel wall. We children used to watch from the safety of the window; terrified we were.

Tom Kelloway obviously enjoyed steady promotion as an expert handler of horses, for the Lopes family were, together with the Drakes, the local gentry. The old schoolroom standing next to Joan's cottage was endowed by Lady Modyford and in 1830 was re-endowed by Sir Massey Lopes. The Lopes family were the successors of Lady Modyford, having purchased her estates from the descendants. The Lopes were the forebears of the present Lord Roborough.

I well remember the move to Buckland, because we had to walk all the way from Horrabridge. The furniture was all brought on a wagon hired from a farm in Horrabridge by my father, and my mother and we children walked behind the wagon. My brother was quite young then, so Mam pushed him in the pushchair, but it was a long way to walk then you know, especially for such little legs, 'cos I was only seven and my sister Barbara was just six. It was the latter part of January, and it was freezing cold with snow on the ground.

We only knew two people when we first came to Buckland to live — my uncle who worked with the butcher and a family from the top of the village called Knott. They had two daughters who were much older than us, and they were sent down to help us move in. We were delighted because they lifted us all up onto the high window-sill in the front room so we could watch the proceedings. It was quite exciting as they had to get a lot of the furniture in through the windows at the front of the cottage because the doors were too small.

In the author's neighbouring cottage there is a similar problem whenever anything large has to be moved up or down the stairs — especially because of the 'lighthouse' spiral stone staircase. Furniture has to be passed throuth a coffin hole — a large area of floor that is easily taken out in sections in one of the bedrooms. This, of course, was also the only way of getting deceased members of the family downstairs, as the name implies. It was probably thought irreverent, to say the least, to pass dead bodies out through the upstairs window if the unfortunate person had died in his or her sleep.

We loved the cottage from the first time we saw it and were thrilled to bits that the school was so close to home. We had so far to go to school at Horrabridge that it was wonderful to be living almost next door to the school. I think that's why Dad took this house so we shouldn't have so far to go.

We were introduced to the cottage by my uncle who was working for Mr Beer the village butcher (where Brook House is now). The landlord was a Mr Palmer in Horrabridge, and when we first moved in he wanted three months' rent taken out to him. Well, I went with my elder sister, Hilda, right up through the fields and over the moor to take this money. Hilda had it in her pocket all wrapped up and do you know what she did? She lost it! Up there on the moor! We searched and searched for that money, because you can imagine how long it had taken to save. The rent was about £12 a year, and my father thought he was well paid at £1 a week, so a quarter of his wages went on the rent. Anyhow, we eventually found the money on the grass, it had dropped out of her pocket, but oh, what a worry it was.

There were four of us children living here, as my brother had been born in Horrabridge in 1909, just before we moved. When we first came to Buckland to live, a Mr and Mrs Stanley lived next door (in the author's cottage) but they moved, and a family called the

Medlands came up from Milton Combe and she had five boys. Another boy, Donald, was born in 1915, the February, and my youngest sister Elizabeth was born in July the same year. We didn't know a baby was coming, but I can remember that awful night when she was born 'cos normally I slept in Mam's room with my brother, and we had to be taken out and put in the other bedroom with my sisters. It was a real squash you know, with the four of us sleeping in there, two to the bottom of the bed and two to the top. Elizabeth was born during the night and my elder sister Hilda was disgusted the next day when she came home for dinner. She kept saying to me:

"I s'pose you've bin up there (school) saying — 'my mother's had a baby, my mother's had a — baby' ".

She was wild about it, probably because she understood what having babies was all about, and I didn't. I didn't even know there was a baby coming and I was twelve! I thought and wondered about Mam getting fatter you know, but it never occurred to me to ask why. We certainly weren't told anything. Of course after I went into service, living with all the other girls, I learnt more about it.

Our cottage only had the two bedrooms. My Mam's bed was right in the corner facing the window and there was a bed for me at one end of the room and one for my brother at the other. There were two little beds in the smaller room for my sisters. Dad joked about the sleeping arrangements when people asked where we all went.

"Oh," he'd say, "When one's asleep I stand him up in the corner and let the others have a turn."

He was always full of fun.

The walls were papered all through the house with thistles and flowers everywhere and the only place not papered was the kitchen where it was very rough with just whitewashed stone walls and flagstone floors which Mam covered with some coconut matting. When Paul and I came here to live after Mam died I can remember digging down the staircase and finding horsehair and all sorts of stuff in the walls . . . the old cob walls. Across the hallway from the kitchen was the front room and the dining room table was in there under the window. We sat on the window-seat to eat our meals, and there were chairs round the rest of the table for the others. We only ever had breakfast in the kitchen, other times we were made to sit at the table proper to eat. The room was crowded with furniture . . . Mam had her little organ in there, and when they had their first wireless Dad put a shelf above the organ for it (that was something wonderful, to have a radio) both Mam and Dad had an easy chair either side of the little grate, and above the fireplace was a small mantelpiece with a big American clock on it, and tiny ornaments on each side. On a table in the corner stood Mam's sewing-machine. I don't know how they got it all in there. That fireplace in the sitting room used to give us some trouble when the chimney needed sweeping. Father would do it himself, after a lot of nagging from Mam. He didn't have any brushes. Now and then he'd borrow some but the traditional way was to use a holly bush. Before we came here the living room had been a post office with a big open hearth. When we swept the chimney we had to take a brick out to get the brush or bush all the way up. Dad would get annoyed because each time he did it, about once a year, he had to take a brick or two out, peel back the wallpaper and then have to redecorate again. But Mam always got on at him to get it done 'cos she was afraid of the wooden beams catching fire.

Next to the front room was what we always called

the 'other room'. In there was a piano, sideboard, easy chairs, and a 'what-not' in the corner which was a pretty little piece of furniture with lots of ornaments on. As for Mam's sideboard, well it was laden with masses of china and bits of silver she had collected over the years, together with the lovely tea-set that the Baring-Goulds gave her as a wedding present.

"SATURDAY NIGHT WAS BATH NIGHT"

CAN YOU IMAGINE what it must have been like to keep a family of five children bathed, washed and generally clean without the aid of a modern bathroom? I, for one, shudder at the very thought of having to haul every drop of water needed to fill a tub, let alone heat it all! What a struggle it must have been for a mother to work in a tiny, overcrowded kitchen, surrounded by boistrous children all reluctantly having a wash. To say nothing of the unpleasant toilet facilities a family such as Joan's had to contend with some seventy years ago. These days to be without a flushing 'loo', running hot and cold water, and a plumbed-in bath is considered unhygienic and the dwelling uninhabitable. Many local councils offer generous improvement grants to have such facilities fitted. A bathroom is no longer considered a luxury, but a necessity. Consider the primitive arrangements for ablutions at Rose Cottage:

We had a great big stool in the kitchen, and on this stool stood a bowl. We'd have to fill up that bowl with water from the bucket kept under the table, and warm it with water from the kettle; there was always a kettle warming on the stove. This was just to have a wash in. I can't ever remember cleaning our teeth though there was a tooth-powder on the market. We never used it but always ate an apple to clean them. There was always plenty of them around.

Saturday night was bath-night — proper ritual it was. The old tin bath would be brought out and put before the fire in the kitchen where it was lovely and warm, and the copper out in the back was lit to heat the water. 'Course every drop had to be fetched specially and we all went in the same water 'else we had to fetch enough water for another bath from the brook! When we had had our baths we all had our toe-nails cut, one after the other. Mam had something made up in a bottle to wash our hair with, like a shampoo but of course there weren't any proprietary brands for sale then. It was some sort of soap powder mixture and it took some time to wash hair with it. There was nothing to make life easy, and 'course we four girls all had long hair down to our waists, so it was quite a job for my poor mother to have to wash that lot. It seemed that every night of our lives she'd sit and comb our hair to look for lice, because it was an awful problem in those days, especially at school with our long hair. It was so easy to pick 'em up. She combed our hair with vinegar and water to get away any nits if she found 'em, and if we moved our heads at all we'd get a real clout with the back of the brush. Then if we wanted our hair to be specially nice for a party or something we got Dad to do our hair, and he'd plait it like he was plaiting the horses manes, really tight. He did that when our hair was wet and then when it had dried it would be all curly. Mam did our hair up in rags for us as well, and that would make it hang down in softer curls. They took a lot of trouble with our hair you know.

Our toilet was at the end of the garden, with the cemetery at the back, and we had a laurel hedge all around to hide it. It was only a wooden seat with a bucket underneath, but when we lived with it no one took any notice 'cause everyone was like it. Indoors we had pots under all the beds and there was a slop-pail out in the back kitchen. Dad had a sort of cess-pit arrangement out in that garden, where this slop-pail together with the bucket from the toilet had to be emptied. Then, in turn, this place was emptied and the contents put over the garden. I don't suppose it was any different to having manure, and my father's said nobody's ever been able to grow rhubarb and cauliflowers since. It was the buckets!

"WASHDAY WAS MONDAY"

"WASHDAY WAS MONDAY, every Monday and all day long!" When Joan said that to me in such a heartfelt way, it brought home just what a hard, thankless slog domestic chores must have been then. Nowadays, thanks to labour-saving devices such as automatically programmed washing-machines and tumble-driers, the housewife's lot has been eased considerably. All we need to do is decide whether to put in one cupful of powder or two, plug in and switch on. Even Joan has conceded to modern machinery by having a spin-drier in her kitchen, although she still does all her washing by hand. When Joan was describing the washday routine to me, I had only just seen the end of having three children in nappies at the same time. What would happen if both washing-machine and drier decided to break down together, or if there was a prolonged power cut? It does not bear thinking about . . . but what about the back-breaking chore of earlier washdays at Rose Cottage . . . ?

First thing would be to get the copper lit out in the back kitchen. It took about ten gallons, which was a lot of water to have to carry from the brook, and it was always brought on Sunday evenings by us children. Mam had a great big wooden tool with two prongs to lift the washing out and Dad always made that for her. He'd get sticks out of the hedge and skin 'em down till they were all white and clean — very primitive, but in them days you had to make do, and make use of anything like that around you. All our rubbish was burned up in that old copper; we saved it up specially; and it would soon have the water boiling merrily. A store of wood was kept out in the back kitchen, and that had to be fetched from the moor. We made sessions of it, with all of us going,

Mam as well, as we'd take our tea with us to have up there. It was lovely wood to burn, the gorse or dry wood where the ponies had trampled it down. Dad cut ferns with the scythe for the pig's bedding and we'd pile all the wood and ferns up and borrow a cart to take them home. It was an outing really . . .

After the copper was lit and going, Mam would be washing all morning. She had two things out there with the copper, the wooden tray her washing was in and a bath down by the side with the 'blue' water in. She only had a bar of soap to rub the clothes on, no powder or anything, but she would put a handful of soda in the copper and something called 'Hudson's Powder'. I'm not sure what that was, but your hand would feel awful after you'd stuck it in, p'raps that was some kind of soda as well. After they were washed all the clothes went into the blue water and she'd wring them out from there. One of us, p'raps when we came home from school to have our dinner, we'd have to be turning the mangle for her. We'd each have a turn, but we didn't mind. Instead of ironing the sheets and things were put through the mangle after they were dried and folded, to get the creases out, and then they'd be all neat. They had to be folded exactly you know, very precisely. Then Mam rubbed a warm flat iron over the folded sheets and this iron was taken out of the fire with tongs so you didn't get burned. The sheets on our beds were yellow because they were made of unbleached calico and Mam boiled them and boiled them so each week they'd get a little whiter.

You can imagine the hectic, steamy chaos of washday and yet, as if she didn't have enough to do, Joan's mother took in washing to make ends meet . . .

There was a house at Crapstone where a Major Phillips lived, and he took in students who were training for the army. Well, Mam, together with Mrs Medland next door washed all the sheets for them. They would be hung up all around our garden to dry and p'raps Hilda or I and one of the Medland boys would take it all back to Crapstone in a flasket (a shallow wicker basket) very big and heavy, it could take eight or nine sheets. We used to quarrel and grumble about having to go back with it 'cos none of us liked doing it.

I've seen my poor mother with sheets up there in the garden blowing in the wind and splitting. They weren't very strong and she'd have to be in the cottage mending them on her little hand sewing-machine before they were sent back. What they had to do then! She only got a about thrupence a sheet, 'twasn't very much, and she shared the money with Mrs Medland!

THE CLOTHES THEY WORE

LOOKING AT the enormous pile of washing about to be stuffed into my trusted, well-used washing machine, I wonder how Joan's mother ever coped with all the white starched linen that her children's clothes were made of. We are spoiled today with all the easy-to-wash synthetic and drip-dry materials on the market. Little girls wear practical warm tights, not the cumbersome, un-comfortable stockings of Joan's childhood. Everything today is neat, comfortable and relatively hardwearing, and we have thank-fully dispensed with the many layers of clothing Joan and her sisters put up with. Imagine, then, the task that must have faced her mother on Monday morning — the endless pile of white aprons, chemises, camisoles, stockings, dresses, bloomers, shirts, and trousers, to say nothing of the other household washing. For the most part, clothes had to be home-made with all the delicately fine needlework that was popular in those days. We wouldn't dream today of sewing well into the night with only flickering candles or dim oil-lamps for light. People took endless care over the finer skill in sewing, and as someone who finds a simple job like putting on a button a chore, I can only admire the care and devotion such needle-work required. We make our children's clothes mainly out of choice, not necessity. For Mrs Kelloway it was a question of economy as Joan herself recounts:

My mother made use of everything because she was very industrious, had to be really. She got her flour delivered in great big sacks of 17½ lbs at a time, and do you know, she cut up those sacks and made our knickers out of them! The sacking was almost like butter muslin, a bit thicker and coarser, but it was yellowy like the Holland material. Well, there was a great big blue circle stamped on the sack, with 'Spillers' Flour' all around it, and Mam boiled and boiled this sacking to get that mark off. My sister Barbara was a monkey, because she would climb the trees, and if anyone was around to see she'd turn up her clothes and show her britches with this 'Spiller's Flour' circle stamp on them! I believe Mam put a bit of embroidery around the bottom of them, to make them a bit prettier, but they were proper knickers you know, right down to our knees. Instead of elastic being at the bottom, they were tied in with a cuff, like bloomers.

Our aprons were always starched and white like the petticoats under our dresses. We might have had these rough britches, but our petticoats were beautiful, with embroidery over them. Under our aprons we wore dresses — I don't think we had jumpers like they do now, you know. There was a dressmaker at Lovecombe Cottage and if Mam was very busy and needed some help with sewing, she would make our dresses. She made us some nice tweed dresses once, the episode always stands out in my memory. Barbara and I were always the same size, as there was only a year and seven months difference in us. Well, Mam would dress us alike and on this occasion we were over by the mounting stone in the village when Lady Drake came by in her carriage. Well, do you know, she called out to us to come over to her and

27

she asked us if we were twins. 'Course we thought this was something wonderful and were delighted to think that Lady Drake had stopped to speak to us. It was a real highlight.

People still wore chemises when I was young, although I don't think we ever wore them. We did have to make them at school though — they were very pretty with embroidery all around the neck and around the sleeves, sort of little half sleeves. You would wear your chemise over your vest, and it was quite long you know. People dressed so differently then, everything was so much longer. The chemise came down like a petticoat and over the top of that you wore your dress, then o'course came the apron — it was a lot to wear. If you didn't wear a chemise then you'd be wearing a camisole, you wouldn't be wearing both. That was like a little bodice and only came down to your waist — we didn't wear bras then, 'twasn't heard of. There were liberty bodices in the winter and they were long with buttoned suspenders at the bottom to keep our thick stockings up.

Whit Sunday was a special time for us because then we'd have a lovely new voile dress of pure white. They were very traditional about things like that you know. Well then, we wore these dresses every Sunday through the summer and I can recall one Sunday in particular. Of course we were wearing our beautiful white dresses, and coming home from Bible Class in Crapstone, a lot of us girls ran down through a cornfield and we didn't stick to the paths! We ran all through the corn and came home with our dresses green! Oh, we had a clip over the ear'ole for that!

My brother wore a smooth velvet suit on Sundays — he looked so smart in it, but he managed to get messed up too, 'cos I remember him falling in the pig's run one Sunday. He did look a sight! He always wore one of those Norfolk jackets with the belt and pleats at the back, little plus-four trousers, and he wouldn't be seen without his old cloth cap, he always wore that.

Mam had an awful time on washdays with Dad's stiff old corduroy trousers 'cos she'd have to scrub and scrub them clean with that horrid soap that never lathered properly. The corduroy was heavier in those days and it had a funny smell about it. Around his trousers Dad had on leather leggings to protect his legs and o'course these collarless shirts and braces.

The thing I remember most about Mam's clothes is her apron, she always had that on. It was a long, white starched apron with a bib up the front, and her dresses were always dark colours, although in the summer I believe she did wear lighter materials. Her hair was scraped up in a bun at the back of her head and she wore those little round-framed glasses.

CHILDREN'S CHORES

IT IS HARD WORK for most modern parents to get their children to do simple chores around the house. Many resort to paying an extra fifty pence or more on top of the expected weekly pocket money in order to get the car cleaned or the grass cut with the help of a motor-mower! We are constantly having to nag the children to wash up, make their own beds, and pick up the debris of scattered toys and games. How much is this due to the fact that many things are now done at the mere touch of a button or flick of a switch — like hoovering the carpet, switching on a light, or plugging in the electric kettle? So little effort is involved in many of the previously time-consuming tasks that perhaps children today can hardly be blamed for their apparent tardiness. The lesson was hard in Joan's young days and there was little room for sympathy. Each child had his or her own daily tasks to fulfill. Heavy loads of washing to carry was just one of them.

The knife-board . . . Oh we hated it! We had to clean the knives on the knife-board with brown emery powder.

One of us had to do the knives, one the spoons and one the forks, and my brother Alf was supposed to clean all the shoes and boots on Saturdays. I say he was supposed to, but he hated it. He'd be out there on the steps grumblin' and would give any of us a penny to do it for him. But we all had our jobs to do. We had to go out in that back kitchen every evening and clean our boots for school the next day, and it was like Greenland out there with that stone floor. We had these hard old boots in a sort of green leather and we had to clean them with blacking, not nice polish that was easy to get off. Oh, we'd be out there rubbing and rubbing to get a shine on them. My Barbara once did a funny thing. She used stove polish! And as she went through the village, Mrs Smith who lived over the road said :

"What 'ave you done maid? Bin cleanin' your boots wi' stove polish?"

'Twas a grey look you see. She thought 'twas lovely 'cos 'twas easier to shine. That was the routine every night and oh, the chilblains we had in the morning! Putting our boots on was real agony.

Now the blackleadin' of the stove was a big job, 'cos the black stove in the kitchen and the grate in the 'other room' both had to be done. My mother would make us turn out every corner and she'd say:

"You turn out the corners, the middle'll take care of itself!"

We had to do it properly.

Each drop of water used in our cottage had to be fetched in buckets and cans from a tap by the brook in the village, and there was always a tub outside the back door to catch rainwater. It was quite an ordeal on Sunday evenings fetching all the water home ready for washing the next day. We'd take it in turns when Mam said:

"Those cans are empty again. If you don't get it that

poor ol' devil'll have to get it soon as he comes in."

That was Dad comin' in from work.

Of course we all had to make our own beds before we went to school in the morning, except washday when the sheets were changed.

When the pig was killed one of our jobs was to clean the belly, you know, the skins. Sometimes we'd go up in the field and clean it because there was always plenty of water in the brook, and I recall one occasion when I was with Barbara cleanin' this belly. Our curate's three children came over to see us. They were called Lettie, Camilia, and Clement, and Barbara was very friendly with Lettie and we felt so ashamed to be over there cleanin' this dirty ol' belly, for them to see us doin' it!

Children were expected to do jobs like that you know. When the goose came from Lew Trenchard we had to go all the way out to Yelverton Station to fetch it. It would

An old view of Buckland Monachorum

31

be left there in a hamper and we'd have to carry it home, and my goodness it was heavy. But it was quite an event for us to go to Yelverton because we'd only go if Mam or Dad wanted something special. There was a butcher's shop, a sweet shop and a flower shop on the corner by Leg O'Mutton, and a bicycle shop where a man would do repairs.

Every morning we had to be up in time to fetch the milk at about half past seven. My sisters and I had to pick it up from where it was left at Netherton House (the farm, only a few hundred yards from the cottage). We had a pennyworth of scald milk which would be about a quart (scald is milk that has been heated and the cream taken off) and we'd have a pint of new milk, all in a jug. Stan Ward was the farmer who used to own all the land round here and provided the milk this end of the village. There were two other farms which supplied milk to the rest of the village. They kept somebody like a maid who brought the milk down to Netherton House for us to collect. (There were a few odd jobs some youngsters could do for which they would be paid a few pence a week.) Up at Crapstone all the water had to be pumped up, and the likes of the older Medland boys each earned a penny or two by going up there every evening and doing so many pumps.

My brother went from here to Coppicetown every morning to get the milk to take right down to a cottage about two miles away and he still had to be back to go to school by nine o'clock . . . for that he'd get about six-pence a week. (For young readers, perhaps it should be pointed out that this was six old pence when there were 240 to the pound.)

A girl in the village, Bertha Crossman, cleaned out the pub before she went to school every morning and she'd get a penny or two for that. Then on Saturdays she would go in and give it a really good scrub out.

CHAPTER THREE

IN THE KITCHEN

If you want a good pudding, to teach you I'm willing
Take two-pennyworth of eggs, when twelve for a shilling.
And the same fruit that Eve had once chosen
Well pared and well chopped, at least half a dozen.
Six ounces of bread, (let your maid eat the crust)
The crumbs must be grated as small as the dust.
Six ounces of currants, the stones you must sort
Lest they break out your teeth, and spoil all your sport.
Six ounces of sugar won't make it too sweet,
Some salt and some nutmeg will make it complete.
Three hours let it boil, without hurry or flutter
And then serve it up without sugar or butter.

Joan Bellan's recipe for her mother's 'Eve Pudding'

THERE WAS MORE to cooking than flicking an electric switch or
lighting a gas ring in Joan's childhood days. Her mother acquired a
weather eye as keen as any sailor's for the art of cooking anything at

all, let alone being able to produce it hot on the table at the re-cognised meal times. It depended on the way the wind was blowing. Joan described the fickle intricacies of old-time baking:

Mam would generally make her cakes when she was doing the Sunday roast, because the fire was right then. The fire had to be just right you see, not too hot or too cold, and she would curse that old stove because it just wouldn't go. I've heard her say on Sunday:

"There's my cake at the top of the pan and me dinner hasn't started, I could sit on that blessed stove!"

Some days there was just no heat in it. It was all to do with the wind and she'd try one door open to give a draught and then she'd try the other, but the fire just wouldn't go — no heat. We'd be sitting here sometimes at tea-time waiting for our dinner to be cooked! You know, we'd come home from church at lunchtime and nothing would have started, poor Mam stood there with her bowl of cake, an earthenware shiny bowl, and the fire would be cold. 'Course there was no other means. I mean, now if that happens you can put the mixture in the fridge to keep for a while, but not then, there was nothing like that. She would study the wind to get the right conditions for the old stove, because she would get so exasperated to be here with all her baking ready to go in.

I can remember going out to Lophill, near Lew-trenchard to see my grandmother and she used a cloam oven. She had an open hearth you see and 'twas a right business getting any baking done in that. She'd have a faggot of wood, like a spray of kindling, lighting wood—and she'd set that alight from the hearth fire. Then the cover was taken off the cloam oven; it looked like sort of white china inside 'cause cloam is a sort of clay; then all that faggot was pushed blazing into the cloam oven. She'd really ram it in and seal it up with the cover back on again. All this wood was taken out with a

34

great big scraper and the oven would then be white hot. The cakes and bread were then put into the oven and sealed up. That's how her cooking was done. The roast dinners we had from that oven were beautiful, there's nothing to beat it today.

My grandmother had four cows as well and she'd go out and milk these cows and make a great big bowl of junket with the milk. From her cream bowl (she made all her own cream of course) she'd lift off the cream on top and put it on top of the junket. It was delicious. You can imagine how it was a treat to go out there and stay. Mam would go with us and we'd stay a few days. This was my father's mother, my mother's mother died when we were quite young. She seemed old to us but she was only sixty-one. My father's mother lived longer and she had one of my dad's sisters living with her, with her two children, so when we went we had a lovely time playing with our cousins. We'd have to go up into the garden and fetch the water from the well, by putting a bucket on the hook and letting it down. I can even recall going to see her for the day and, my goodness, what a journey it was. My brother would have to be in a pushchair, and we'd walk to Horrabridge Station, take a train to Tavistock, and then change to the other station at Tavistock. That meant walking right over the other side of the town—it was called North Station. We'd get another train there to Coryton and then walk four miles to Lophill. And we did all that in a day and back.

It is fair to say that, in the country at least, most housewives still make their own cakes and pastries, but there is an important difference in the way we make them. I, for one, take full advantage of modern gadgetry like food mixers and liquidizers, which save precious time in the kitchen. Many of us are the proud owners of a deep-freeze, enabling us to bake and buy in bulk, and there is the convenience of the constant availability of items such as self-raising flour, finely ground with the useful additives of bicarbonate of soda

The baker's van about 1940

and cream of tartar (commonly known as baking powder). We can buy soft margarine so that the housewife who does not possess a mixer can at least save herself the arm-breaking slog of creaming-in hard old fat to make a super-light sponge. I realised while talking to Joan, that most of our cakes today are sponge cakes, but:

There was never much fat in the cakes Mam made, they were all yeast cakes; I don't think she made sponge cakes much. Of course there wasn't such a thing as margarine then you know and butter was so scarce and expensive you couldn't use it to put in a cake. No, Mam'd make these yeast cakes once a week, three big cakes and buns to go on with. She'd get her yeast from the baker, a Mr Caramel, who came down to the village with his bread two or three times a week from Horrabridge. We always called our cakes after the railway stations near here, and we'd count the currants and say 'Horrabridge, Yelverton, Tavistock, Marsh Mills . . . '; it was railway station cake!

I can remember my own children coming with me to visit Mam much later on, and they'd be offered a bit of Nana's cake and it would be so stale they'd chuck it over the hedge because it'd be some that she wanted to get rid of. She wouldn't use this week's cake before last week's was gone, that's how she lived you see and that's how we had to live.

Mam made 'potato cake' a lot and o'course she always made her pasties and pies. She was a beautiful crimper and made lovely pasties, often winning prizes at the flower shows you know. Her pasties were chiefly 'tiddy and point' (potato and meat) and with the 'tiddy and point' Mam put turnip and onion. We were always given our turnips by the farmers then, you never had a turnip weighed like you do now, and of course the onion came from the garden so it was a really cheap meal—the 'point' being very sparse. We ate a lot of turnip greens,

37

especially in the winter time, but you don't see them being eaten much now do you?

When a pig had been killed there was more meat about and Mam would make a round pie then with parsley in it. It was like an egg and bacon pie with a crust on top of it.

There was always a rice pudding or a bread pudding—we called that 'Nelson Squares'. It was made with all the stale bread soaked and spiced, and then mixed with fruit and a little suet and baked in a baking tin. Then you could eat it hot or cold cut up in squares.

White blancmange was a favourite of ours, and Mam flavoured it with a couple of laurel leaves from off the hedge around the privvy. The taste was rather like that of almond. People don't use things like that now do they? Well I s'pose they don't have to, everything is provided in packets now, but people like Mam had to be so much more resourceful. She used mint a lot as a flavouring as well because it was so available.

RECIPES

HERE ARE SOME of Mrs Kelloway's recipes:

KETTLE BROTH
(For breakfast or supper)
A cupful of stale bread
Cover with boiling water and a knob of butter
Season it with salt and pepper and a little milk.

BREAD PUDDING
About ½ lb stale bread (soaked)
2 oz. suet
Few raisins, currants or sultanas
1 teaspoon mixed spice
Pinch of nutmeg
Mix together with milk and bake until golden brown
This is nice to eat cold

POTATO CAKE
½ lb mashed potatoes
1 oz fat
3 oz flour
½ teaspoon baking powder
Pinch salt

Mix all the ingredients together with milk
Roll out and bake for 15-20 minutes

PASTIES
1 lb flour
6 oz fat
Water to mix pastry

Filling
Beef and kidney or pork cut up
Raw potato cut up
Turnip cut up
Onion cut up

Mix together with salt and pepper and flour, with a little water in a bowl. Roll the pastry into rounds, cut to the size required using a plate. Place the mixture in the middle and bring the sides to meet the top. Crimp along the seam, after moistening the edges with water. Brush the top with milk or beaten egg.

YEAST CAKE
2 lbs flour
½ lb fat
½ lb currants
Strained saffron (soaked overnight)
1 oz yeast
½ pint warm milk
6 oz sugar

Mix yeast with a little sugar taken from the 6 oz until it froths. Mix altogether until it doubles in size. Put into cake tin or make into buns. Prove for ten minutes and then bake in a very hot oven.

ISLE OF WIGHT JAM
4 lbs rhubarb
6 lbs sugar
2 oz lemon peel
2 oz citron peel
2 oz almonds
2 lemons
2 oranges

Boil oranges and lemons in enough water to cover until quite soft. Strain off water. Cut up all ingredients very small. Add about 1 pint of liquor. Boil 1 to 1½ hours until it thickens. Put into warm jars and tie down.

WINE-MAKING

WINE-MAKING is now a popular hobby for many people, with specially-prepared kits available in any department store, together with the most elaborate-looking equipment that, we are assured, is essential for home brewing.

None of this was thought of for Joan's mother, who, like most cottagers of her time, made all her own wine.

Hers was the most basic equipment, tested by time. There were no supermarket shelves crammed with cheap 'plonk' then, and wine, far from being an everyday drink, was made by the womenfolk for their own consumption on special occasions. But it was also popular with the men . . .

My mother used to make wine and of course I've told you how my father used to like his drink. Well, the wine was kept in an enormous cupboard in the passage, and every so often a bottle or two would go missing! Poor ol' Mam kept wondering where it was and, do you know, my Dad would take a bottle of her wine when he was hard up for a drink and he'd sneak up to the privvy and hide the empties in the laurel hedge round the privvy! We laughed and laughed about Dad taking these bottles away and Mam finding them empty, hidden in the hedge! I think 'twas only ever blackberry wine 'cos Mam didn't go in for different sorts like we do today. (Probably because the abundant hedgerows within a convenient walk of Rose Cottage provided more than enough berries each autumn.)

It was a traditional thing to make wine; she'd like to have it around for Christmas time, or if anyone came in. 'Twas a special occasion drink and it was s'posed to 'ave bin kept, but of course my father kept taking it! We never saw him do it you know, but Mam would find an empty bottle and she'd say:

"That ol' devil's had it again!" when she went to get a bottle of wine from her cupboard and it wasn't there.

I don't think we were allowed to have wine to drink then, we didn't have intoxicating stuff. Mam made this ginger wine for us children with a ginger plant. When she'd made her plant, it would have to be left for a certain length of time before she put it all in a big bowl with more water. The next step was to bottle it all up. 'Twas proper ginger beer, you know, and that was our treat.

Of course they didn't have all these traps and things to make their wine with then. Mam had a big brown stain, which was an earthenware bowl, a big open-topped one all shiny inside (like the one she salted the pig in). Well she'd put the fruit, water, sugar and yeast into this stain and the mixture was left to simmer and stand for a month—all covered with muslin and tied down. Then as the wine gradually subsided in the stain, she'd strain it off and bottle it. You'd soon know if she'd put the corks on too soon 'cos they'd blow off with a big bang.

CHAPTER FOUR

CHARMERS, PIXIES, AND SUPERSTITIONS

WHEN JOAN was born into the age of the horse, the scythe, and the cloam oven at the turn of the century, many important tasks on the land and in the home were only undertaken when the signs were right. Sowing, planting, and harvesting were dictated not only by the seasons, but by a jumble of age-old primitive beliefs. Even some domestic chores could only be tackled at certain times, sometimes for totally inexplicable reasons, for people had long since forgotten the pagan logic behind the 'do's and don'ts' of the countryside. Although science and mechanisation have in Mrs Bellan's life-span taken over to a baffling degree, local customs and folklore still linger on, and not just in the memory of village elders like herself. There are little rituals she and other locals observe, and great store is put in several remedies passed down by her mother's generation.

42

Joan is happy to benefit these days from the doctors, nurses and new-fangled equipment at our lovely health centre in nearby Yelverton, but she readily admitted to believing in the mysterious powers of charmers . . .

Now people run off to the doctor for the slightest little thing . . . we didn't have the doctors to go to . . .

I knew a farmer at Axtown (a mile or so from the village) who used to do charming and he could stop bleeding or treat burns. If people would tell him there was somebody having a haemorrhage—even if they weren't there—he could stop it. It was a secret sort of prayer or something he said. I took Eric (my son) to him once 'cos he'd done something like burning his hand on the stove, well this man charmed it and Eric never even had a blister. He would never let anyone know the charms but passed it on to his daughter, because he couldn't pass it on to a male. She in turn couldn't tell a female, so she passed it on to her husband. He only died about twelve months ago, and I have heard that he passed the charm on to his daughter-in-law, and she to her son . . . they're called Germans but where they live now I don't know.[4]

He could get rid of warts, too, by saying a charm, but again he'd never let on what he had said. I remember once I took Paul to a charmer 'cos he had a bad place on his leg. It had been going on and on and wouldn't clear up—'twas really nasty. Well, a friend told me of this farmer's wife out on Dartmoor, at Two Bridges it was, and said she could cure it. This woman looked at Paul's leg and said: "You must go to a doctor, I can't do anything to that."

She was right in a way 'cos it turned out to be an ulcer and Paul was a long time going back and forth to the doctors and hospital having it seen to. Jackie (Joan's daughter-in-law) had a lot of warts on her hand and so did Keith (her grandson), so while I was with this charmer I gave her their names and addresses, because she said

Joan, about 1920

she could cure them without seeing them. Well, the warts did eventually go, but I don't think it was because of the charmer. My friend believed in this charmer woman because her dogs got very bad eczema and she used to make them better . . . the vet charged pounds to do it!

When I was a girl there was a man called Georgie Moses and he was a charmer in the village. He sat on the bridge by the pub and if you had warts he told you to cut a potato in half and rub it on the warts, and then bury it in the garden. They said that as the potato rotted so did the wart. I can picture that old man now, a funny character he was, mind you, there were strange folk round then . . .[5]

The little people feature in folklore all over the world and particularly in Celtic regions, so it was no surprise when Joan had one small tale to tell about Devon's famous pixies:

My father used to tell us there were pixies in a field on the way to Milton Combe and we would walk through there to get to church or chapel in that village. It was while Dad was working in Lopwell when I was about ten . . . [6]

There are other local pixie stories: 'One of the inhabitants of the Gift House (the local almshouse) said a woman while crossing Oxted Park got "mazed" and when she recovered her senses she found herself in another part of the parish, having been pixie-led. Also an elderly Milton Combe man declared that he had been pixie-led in the same field and only recovered his senses by turning his coat inside out. This seems to be a general superstition.'[7]

Yet there is also bad luck involved, it seems, in inverting clothing. According to Joan:

If you put anything on inside out you mustn't change it back. It's unlucky, d'you see. I would feel like that now—the other day I wore my petticoat inside out all day 'cos I'd put it on wrong—I wouldn't change it.

45

I've heard that a bird falling down a chimney is bad luck as well. And a robin—when a robin sings outside your door it's a bad omen, a death or something just as bad will happen. My mother would say "that robin's singing again" and I bet we'd hear of somebody who'd died!

This must be an unnerving superstition for many readers who, like me, have always been taught to regard the robin as a welcome, cheerful little bird. Perhaps one could understand it more if the bird involved was supposed to be a big black crow, or something more ominous.

My Dad used to say "when I'm gone and that blackbird's singing, you'll know it's me come back." You know how beautifully they sing, and often when I'm in that cemetery (which is right behind Joan's garden) and I see a lovely blackbird I think of him . . .

A girl I knew turned a knife up on its side one day and it stayed there. So she said "whenever you see a knife like that think of me." Well, she died; she was having her first baby and she died, 'twas very sad, but I couldn't stop thinking of her. Even if I saw a knife like it now I'd think of her you know; 'twas many years ago.

I don't wash blankets in May and neither does any of my family—or else you defy superstition. If mine isn't done in April then they have to wait till June. And you mustn't wash on a bank holiday or you'll wash one of your family away, or Innocents' Day—that's another day you shouldn't do the washing. It wouldn't matter on St Stephen's Day, but Innocents' Day,the day after . . . If Mam found herself ready to wash on Innocents' Day, it had to be put off.

They say shoes'll pinch if you wear someone else's. People would never pass shoes and boots down in the family because of that, although in them days people were glad to pass down all manner of things . . . You must never put an umbrella up in the house . . . if you see coal lying on the ground you must pick it up and put it in the first fire you come to . . . anybody's house, it didn't matter. If I saw a lump o'coal now on the ground I'd pick it up and put it on the fire. It's something we've always done, you see.

REMEDIES

Joan's BLACKCURRANT TEA   for a cold
Three tablespoons of blackcurrant jam
1 pint of boiling water
A little lemon juice
Stand for ten minutes, strain and drink hot.

A SIMILAR REMEDY is made by collecting elderflowers. Dry them, add boiling water, a little lemon juice and sugar.

Linseed boiled with liquorice was another concoction drunk to ward off coughs and colds. Linseed was also used in hot poultices for septic wounds, to draw out the poison.

In these pill-popping days, it is hard to imagine how people managed to do without. We have instant relief for most minor ills like headaches, indigestion, tummy upsets, eye strain, or spots. Joan's childhood might have lacked the countless bottles of pills and potions readily available at any chemist's shop, but it did have its own set of country remedies for many ailments . . .

Do you know I never had an asprin? I didn't know what a painkiller was and I used to have awful migraine at school. Very often I had to sit out in the porch 'cos I couldn't bear to be in the classroom, and I've been out there ever such a long time, until it was home time. I wouldn't be allowed to come home early, just had to sit in that porch—it was like a cloakroom. They called it sick-headaches, but of course it was migraine.

We used to put nutmeg in our pockets for rheumatism and an acorn in the bed for cramp. I can remember putting an onion in a bucket of water to take away the smell of paint. A nutmeg in the pocket will keep away the toothache as well . . . Ol' Jim Fox across the road (retired carpenter who lived in a cottage opposite Joan) said to me that he had to keep his side of the bed all right 'cos if he went over to his wife's side he was lying on a load of nutmegs! They was everywhere!

This conjures up a comical scene. What with the bedclothes cluttered up with nuts it's a wonder a body could sleep, but Joan can offer no country cure for insomnia![8]

You use a 'blue bag' or vinegar for bee stings and something alkaline for wasp stings. People don't seem to use a blue bag much these days but we always rinsed our whites in the blue.

The milky juice of a weed—the petty spurge—was rubbed on a wart. It healed one of mine, but it had to be this particular weed with a tiny yellow flower. It was very common, but you have to hunt for it today.

Mam used to give us brimstone and treacle for spots, which we didn't mind really, mind we didn't like it too powdery, you want to mix it up well. We would be given that for three mornings, then leave it off for three mornings and then have it again for three.

Another thing we looked for was wild sage, which we steeped in boiling water and made a tea which we drank for three mornings, then dropped it for three mornings.[9]

There were also some 'not so nice' complaints that were not so magically disposed of . . . my sister Barbara used to get terribly constipated and my mother would get a bar of soap. I've seen her put on a 'rubber finger' and then put the soap up her behind. That used to do it!

48

Children got worms a lot, tape worms, and there's no end to them once they start. I believe it was poor Barbara who had tape worms. I don't know how Mam dealt with it but it all had to be got rid of . . . I expect she went up to the nurse at Crapstone.

Joan's prevention against rheumatism was:

Epsom salts, a lemon and a pint of boiling water. Cut the lemon up, pith and skin an' all and add 1 oz of Epsom salts. If you drink a wineglass of that every morning it'll help keep the rheumatism away.

For a cut that was bleeding we'd put a bunch of cobwebs on it. I've done that many times, 'cos there are always cobwebs in the house aren't there? These remedies always worked—and it was often the only thing we had . . .

There was a major lived locally and he used to say: "If I saw my niece with powder and lipstick on I should think she was a disreputable character."

It wasn't done in those days, but a few cosmetic things like rinses were used. I think they used henna rinses.

It's not surprising village folk didn't go running off to the doctor every time they sneezed. One reason why the old country cures survived even with the advent of modern medicine was probably because it took too much effort, time, and money. The sick only resorted to the doctor when the pain was too great to endure or the ailment persisted and defied the various witches' brews.

We had to walk to Horrabridge to see a doctor, and a dentist used to come once a week. We had to walk out there if we wanted a tooth pulled (two or three miles; a trek even when healthy. Imagine plodding through the rain or snow with a throbbing jaw!) There was nothing here in Buckland . . . I have heard my father say the blacksmith would come

49

Joan and Paul Bellan on their Golden Wedding Day

down here on this green outside and pull teeth. Awful thought! The village green has long since been covered by the row of houses directly in front of the church.

The ordeal in Joan's day took place at Horrabridge in someone's sitting-room, which the dentist used to hire. The dentist, Mr Edmunds, charged about 2s. 6d. The doctor at Horrabridge was called Dr Revel and he lived at The Retreat. According to Joan:

People walked there; the only conveyance if you could afford it was a Mr Pike and his jingle and pony. A school doctor would come about once every six months, and I can remember one of my sisters having to have her tonsils out. My mother went off with her to Yelverton station in the jingle and she had to leave Hilda in the hospital in Plymouth. She had her tonsils out and then the same evening, quite late, she was brought home in the jingle with her throat all done up. The same day: you had to be tough in them days!

Joan chuckled at the memory of the old doctor when, on her Golden Wedding Anniversary, she and Paul were chauffeur-driven in style for a celebration meal at the Retreat—now a hotel.

INFANT MORTALITY

The great Jehova full of love
A messenger did send
To call this little babe above
To joys that never end.[10]

WHEN JOAN KELLOWAY and her sisters and brother came into the world, chances of survival beyond childhood were much slimmer than today. It was a common sight to see tiny coffins being borne into Buckland Church, and even young children were expected to share the grief.

Joan recalled one such sad occasion:

I had a particular friend with baby twin brothers who were six months old called Cecil and Cyril. Cecil died, and I had to be one of the bearers who took that little white coffin to the cemetery. 'Twas so sad.

People lived in fear of epidemics, and Joan's neighbour, Jim Fox, recalled thankfully that his family survived intact an infamous outbreak of 'flu. Joan's memories of this are vivid, and tinged with sorrow:

It was an awfully black time really—1919, just at the end of the war. It was the worst epidemic I've ever seen and it took a lot of lives. I was in service at the time and the nurse there had the 'flu very badly. She was so ill that they called her father to be with her; Hilda was her name.

He was a very religious man, praying all the time, and the lady of the house took me in to see Hilda, as she kept asking for me. I didn't realise that she was so ill and dying, and she looked at me with her feverish eyes and was rambling:

"Don't stay here Joan, don't stay here. They're killing me and they'll kill you too."

Well, she terrified me, and after that I had bad dreams and would run out of my room screaming, and they'd have to take me back to bed. Hilda died in the end, and the morning afterwards, her father, a little tiny man, he was, came down and said:

"I'm rejoicing, I'm rejoicing, I've thrown away my sackcloth and ashes."

It preyed on my mind. He was like a religious fanatic, but I was so sad that she had died, I couldn't understand his rejoicing.

My brother-in-law's brother and sister both died of the 'flu and they were only five and three years old. My mother and father were also ill with it, and I would come down and see them and help out at home. They were very lucky because they both recovered.

When I was very young, about two, and we were still living in Tavistock I can remember Hilda who was four having diptheria. She was kept in a small bed in the corner of the room surrounded by a screen of sheets soaked in disinfectant to keep germs from the rest of the family. It's a wonder none of the rest of us caught it. Little Barbara was only four months old and still being nursed. Hilda recovered and was left paralysed for some time.

With home confinements the rule rather than the exception and no expert medical help immediately to hand, it was no surprise that many babies were lucky to survive childbirth or the first few vital weeks of life.

I've heard them talk in the village, my mother and all her friends, how the midwives used to go out, not proper midwives like today, but old ladies who were always the ones who had the knowledge to go out and deliver a child. That's how there were so many that died I suppose. They'd all be born at home, there was no other place. When I was a child Mrs Brown, one of the old ladies who lived in the Gift House, used to deliver babies.

CHAPTER FIVE

"THE GAMES WE PLAYED"

MODERN PARENTS are absorbed in the complex nature of their children's minds and are constantly encouraged to follow the teachings of various child psychologists. It is a wonder our children grow up as well-balanced as they do! However, in the days of Joan's childhood, little, if any, attention was paid to the stimulation a young child might need, or to his or her personal problems, fears, pleasures and expectations. Yet children then were not bored, and neither was there the plague of nervous disorders and phobias brought on by the hectic pace of modern living. They were content, spending many a happy hour creating their own amusements, unaided by the barrage of toys enjoyed by children now. The selection of toys and games for the modern child is quite overwhelming,and perhaps it can be said that the boredom of many of today's children is the result of not being encouraged to think for themselves, that they rely too heavily upon the sophisticated gadgets marketed to amuse them. Not many children of Joan's generation grew up 'delinquent' and she herself was certainly not bored, as she says:

We were contented, you know, although we didn't have the toys they do now. We played a lot with the Medland boys from next door, but we didn't get together much as families—there were six boys you know, and five of us—but we used to play together, mind, in the evening after school when our jobs were done. We played a lot in the back garden and I can remember once when my mother and Mrs Medland had gone to a Mothers' Union meeting together my sister somehow strung up a swing over a tree. Well, I was playing on this swing and I fell off. I broke my thumb, and I was in agony with it, but all I kept saying was "Don't tell Mummy, don't tell Mummy".

Anyway, when my mother came home, she took me up to the nurse at Crapstone, and she bound it. But that thumb never set properly and hasn't been straight since.

We used to go up in Church Meadow (the field next to the school) and play for hours climbing the trees up there. We had one tree in particular that we called our 'ocean' and we each had a seat in it. My sister Barbara was a monkey. She had what we called an 'apple coat', which was a coat that had a loose lining sewed all around at the bottom. Well, she used to go into the orchard near our cottage and steal the apples, putting them in the lining of this coat. She was never encouraged to do it, but she was always the daring one of the family. Another prank of hers was to take one of the blue paper sugar bags to school wi' her and then run off in the dinner hour (there were no school dinners then you know) down the road, over the hedge into this orchard and fill it up with

55

apples. Then she'd take them back to Church Meadow to our tree, and we'd sit there in our 'ocean' eating these apples. My mother caught her at it once and she made Barbara take each and every one of those apples back to the orchard. She was very angry,and I believe Barbara got a clout for her sins! A game we played a lot was 'Two's and Three's', where a boy stood in the middle and all the other children stood in doubles round him. Then they called out 'Fire on the mountain, run, run, run,' and the outside ring would run. Once when we were playing this game, there was a boy called Charlie Knott in the middle—he had a terrible stutter. Anyway, we all ran, he shouted "Fire's out" and do you know what he did? He started to wee all over everyone!

We had a doll each and a doll's pram between us that someone had given us. My doll was a wooden one with a wax face, and it was left out in the sun one day. Well of course the wax melted and Mam put it in the doll's pram in the other room, but I was afraid to pass that door and look at this doll; it looked terrifying, so I hated it. Later on we had dolls that were all wooden and they were much tougher. We played things like marbles and hopscotch of course, but those sort of games are timeless aren't they? We had wooden hoops as well, with a stick to make 'em go, but the boys always had an iron hoop.

Cherry time was lovely because we all sat out on the step playing 'cherry hop, cherry hop'. The others had to guess how many cherries I'd got in my hand and then they'd take a turn.

A favourite pastime was to go up in the old privvy and burn all the cobwebs with a candle. It's a wonder we never burnt the place down! We loved to get out of the house and go up there. Of course there were cobwebs everywhere, and we always had candles. Well, they don't let children have candles now.

Joan went on to tell me of some of the escapades she and her brother and sisters got up to as children. They were fairly harmless childish pranks and she related them, chuckling at the memory:

There was some game here Guy Fawkes' Night because we'd tie people's door handles together and put squibs (fireworks) under their door. My brother would walk to Horrabridge to get these squibs and they made a lovely bang. Anyone we held a grudge against had one under their door. I know we tantalised Bill and Sophie Hawkins something terrible like that.

When the baker came into the village selling his bread, we had a lovely time with his baskets, especially in the winter when the ice came. We used to pinch his baskets and take them to the meadow and sit in them, sliding down the ice. We had a whale of a time, with the baker on the hedge shouting at us, and we'd be down the bottom with his baskets, sitting in them!

We used to play in the brook, and when father was walking past one day he spied young Barbara in the middle making mud pies. He told her to come out but the cheeky monkey said she would come when she was ready. He marched her all the way home and took his buckle strap to her. You'd expect to be punished for being disobedient. We were allowed out in the evenings but Mam would be standing like a sentry on the doorstep and if we were late back she'd give us a clip round the ear.

We never seemed to want for anything to do in those days, you know. Children then always seemed to make their own games, or we were happy just to sit on the steps crocheting or knitting. There was always so much time; no television was there?

LEISURE TIME

PUSH-BUTTON ENTERTAINMENT like television and radio dominates much of our leisure time these days, but in Joan's childhood a family had to rely completely upon its own resources—books and music in particular. It is only when we have a power failure that we realise how very differently spare time was spent then. Dinner parties were the prerogative of the upper classes and probably because of the cost and space involved, cottagers did not entertain much at home. As Mrs Bellan explains, there was not much room for outsiders during their cosy evenings round the fire:

It was always the family, we never had friends in and entertained like they do now. We were enough in those days. You youngsters are always going into other people's homes. Every Sunday we had long evenings at home, with my mother playing the organ—she couldn't get on with the piano although we had it here. She had cared for that organ since she was ten years old, and when she died my sister had it made into a writing-bureau; it's beautiful wood. We'd sing all the Sankey hymns from the book, with Mam reading the music, things like 'The Old Rugged Cross', 'All His Jewels', and 'Trust and Obey', and Dad sang little ditties to us like 'Two Little Girls in Blue' and 'Daddy, Dear Daddy'. We had lovely evenings singing, because we all loved music, and gradually each one of us in turn learned to play the piano. Hilda could play anything by ear and Barbara was quite good at playing. Mrs Beer from Crapstone taught her to play, and as Mam couldn't afford to let her have a whole hour she just had half. Later on as I got older I wanted to learn, and as I was earning my own money I started lessons. I only had them for about two years, but as Elizabeth grew up I paid for her to have them. She got on really well, and played the church organ in time, and became the deputy organist. We were a musical family you know; my mother had a brother in

Torquay who played the violin and when we were all together we had lovely sing-songs. Barbara and I sometimes went to Torquay on the train to see him, and we'd have to walk to Horrabridge, get a train to Plymouth, change there for Newton Abbot and then change again for Torquay. It was quite a journey, and we hated it when the train went through a tunnel. We'd have about two weeks in Torquay—quite a holiday!

At home we went to bed fairly early, and when we were all upstairs my sister Hilda was allowed to read to us before we got into bed. There was always a chair between the two bedrooms and we all knelt round her sitting there. If there was any word that she couldn't say or that she didn't understand, she used to say 'Jerusalem', and we always knew that that was the wrong word, and try to find out what it should really be. Hilda read nice books to us—our Sunday School prizes or school prizes, usually a Bible, a Tennyson or Grimms Fairy Tales. After Hilda had finished reading to us Mam came up and heard us say our prayers, and oh my, we always said our prayers! The same one was said every night:

> Gentle Jesus, meek and mild
> Look upon this little child
> Pity my simplicity
> Suffer me to come to Thee.

And of course we prayed for our family and friends: then we said:

> Jesu my Lord I Thee adore
> Oh make me love Thee more and more

Lastly we said the Lord's Prayer. That was the routine every single night.

The advent of cars and buses has considerably extended the entertainment possibilities for everyone, and it is this mobility that is the largest factor in widening the scope of leisure activities. Nothing is thought of driving many miles to go to the cinema, to visit friends for an evening, or just go to a pub, but for someone like Joan's parents there was no life outside the village itself, as Joan recounts:

There wasn't much entertainment outside the home, it was work and home really, although my father did like to go to the pub in the village sometimes. He got a pound in wages (and that was good pay in those days) and some of it got taken to the pub. Mam would look out across to the pub and she'd say:
"Your father's back, but his bike's over there."
He liked to go across and have a drink and 'course he always had his cider out in the back. They made the cider at a pound at Coppicetown, and all the apples in the orchards were taken up there. It's all gone now of course, over in the orchard here you'd see a mountain of apples piled high in two or three lots, and there'd be old pigs in there with 'em, and horses and cows. Then the men would come and shovel the apples up into the carts and take them up to the cider pound. Well, Dad liked his drink of cider and I've heard my brother say how he would go up with him to get a barrel—a little barrel of four and a half gallons— and then let the barrel roll all the way down the road to save carrying it. Cider was all people drank then and they used to say it made you drunk; well, you don't have cider like it now do you? We'd see Mr Ward, who supplied us with our milk, having his breakfast drink every morning, and it'd be a pint of cider, with all the ropey old stuff hanging off it.

The 'ropey' stuff Joan refers to was probably just apple bits—or was it? West Country cider folklore is full of tales about the incredible magic ingredients slipped into barrels of scrumpy to give it a unique flavour. Rusty chains, a bit of raw meat, even a dead rat was often slipped in on the quiet, if you believe the stories.

The Manor Inn

The only other simple pleasure Joan's father enjoyed was his weekly wad of tobacco.

Dad also had his pipe but I don't suppose it was very expensive. I think Mam had what she was supposed to but with times bad and four or five of us children to feed it wasn't very easy. He had to slice his tobacco up with a knife because it came in blocks.

FEASTS AND FESTIVALS

WITH SO LITTLE to relieve the mundane everyday life of cottagers it is no wonder that much was made of annual festivals like Christmas, Easter and Harvest Festival. Preparations were intense, involving the whole family, and although there were no Christmas cards sold as early as September, or Easter eggs beautifully packaged in colourful foil, care and thought went into the planning of these special occasions. There was little money to spend on extras but this did not restrict the pleasure of everyone. Each person contributed to the occasion, whether it was a family or a village affair, as Joan remembers :

Christmas was always an occasion, because there was always so much planning and extra work to be done. We would all sit around the table in the other room getting the fruit ready for my mother to make the pudings—like stoning the raisons and scraping the suet, or chopping it with a knife. There was nothing handy—no implements to help you do any of the jobs. No, it was long and slow, but we all enjoyed it 'cos we all did it together. We'd have to scrape the orange as well, but we didn't mind that 'cause it was the only time of the year that we ever saw an orange, they were very scarce. We'd have one in our stockings, and oh, we did love them. We had a few nuts and dates or figs and some sweets and then it was a treat wasn't it? We three girls had a wooden doll each, and every year my mam would make new dresses for our dolls. That was our Christmas present. I can remember one year in particular when we were given a bat and shuttlecock. 'Twas wonderful to have that, and we'd play with our friends with this bat and shuttlecock and it was always getting stuck in the hedge around our garden.

We had nice Christmases, but there weren't many of us. I mean our aunts and uncles lived away and weren't near enough to come.

We were very fond of my mother's younger sister and she came to stay with us for Christmas—that was a highlight you know, to have her come and stay. But then she got married and had seven children of her own!

We didn't even get together with the Medlands much as there were so many of us, but Mam always sent in a piece of her pudding and Mrs Medland would send back a piece of hers. Just to taste. We would buy Mam a little box of hairpins, or something like that, between us as we had no money to buy anything really. There were always gifts taken for the hospital at Christmas time, by the Church, and we went carol-singing with the Sunday School holding a collection tin. We held lanterns as well, but we were never asked in for something to eat or drink like they are now. I suppose they didn't have it to do it with then, you know. There weren't many gentry about. I can remember going up to the Vicarage and being given some soup, with old Mrs Haynes (the Vicar's wife) stood at the top of the steps ladling it out to us. At Easter-time we'd have an 'egg' service, where the children took gifts for the hospital to the Church, either proper eggs or chocolate eggs. It was something that was always done and it was a great ceremony taking these eggs up to the front of the Church. The children loved it.[11]

It is sad that there are now no working farms left in the centre of the village. In Joan's time there were at least two in the village itself; but a farm then could exist on a few cows, seven or eight being a large herd, according to Joan. Harvest Festival was a much bigger occasion in a farming village when the seasons of the year were all-important. Buckland did not have one Harvest Home for all the village folk, but rather each farm had its own, after the threshing was completed.

My father always helped with the threshing; everyone did, it was all hands to the pump. There were no machines then you see, so the farmers relied on the men of the village to help with the harvest, 'cos that was the only way to get the corn. I can remember being in the harvest field stooking the corn when I was quite a young child. Most of the children went up there to help because we were useful, and there was nothing else to do was there?

After I was married I often helped with Harvest Homes because Paul was always called to make the hay ricks. He was an excellent rick-maker and he'd be on the rick making it, while the other men were pitching. The thresher went round each farm in turn to thresh the corn gathered in the barn, and all the farmers in the district helped each other out. They'd be at one farm one day, then another, and after each farm had finished the farmer's wife would give a huge lunch for all the men who had helped. There'd be a huge leg o' pork or salt beef, potatoes and always turnip and 'flatpoll' or cow cabbage (put for feeding of cows) but she'd give it for their lunch. Farmers never had a garden for themselves. When I went to help with the lunches I was shocked because the pudding (usually a big suet one) was served on the plates they'd eaten their meat off, to save on washing up! That was the Harvest Home.

It wasn't just these seasonal festivities which made a special occasion. Anything which broke the mundane routine was welcomed and one such occasion stands out in Mrs Bellan's memory as being particularly exciting.

In 1915 King George and Queen Mary spent a night at Horrabridge Station in their train, and we went to see the train go through. It stood in a siding, and as we weren't allowed anywhere near the railway crossing, we stood on the bank to catch a glimpse of them. I can well remember walking down over the moor with our Mam to be there in time. It was evening time, after school, and the crowd was really big, and we all had little paper Union Jacks to wave. I think the King and Queen were going to inspect the troops and we caught a glimpse of her waving to us through window. She had a 'toque' hat sitting on her head, with the scarf coming down from the hat and tying underneath. My mother had one when she was married, a white hat and gloves and a pretty blue dress. I don't think people stuck so much to the white wedding then—'twasn't a practical colour was it? But seeing the King and Queen was very exciting and I'll never forget it.[12]

Another thing we always did was have a tea party in the summer, and different people in the village would let us use their gardens for it. We often went up to Major Bunduck's at Uppaton and all the children marched behind the band all the way up the lane you know, to the tea party.

They played things like 'Rule Brittania' and old Bill Hawkins played the big trombone, a great big fat man he was! Mr Pike was in the band as well, but my father wasn't in it, he couldn't play anything like that. We had the most lovely tea party with sideshows, games, and activities arranged for us. As time went on the band disbanded and all the instruments were kept hanging in a net in the cloakroom of the school. They were there for years, but I don't know what happened to them then, I suppose they were all sold.

One of the grand events in the village during Joan's childhood was the annual flower show and sports day, interrupted only by the two wars. It is still a major annual happening in the life of Buckland, now called the 'Buckland Summer Fair', one of the largest and best attended country fairs in the area. Nearly all the able-bodied villagers are involved in something to do with the fair, which is held in the grounds of Pound House, home of Lord and Lady Morley, about a mile away from the village centre.

In the last couple of years the fair has been staged in the main street of the village itself with crowds of visitors passing Joan Bellan's front door. Buckland is closed to traffic for the day and the locals end up dancing into the night in the street—not such a far cry from the fairs recalled by Joan.

Several thousand people attend the fair every year and thousands of pounds have been raised for charities and local organisations.

The Flower Show was always held on the first Wednesday of August, and it was a big event in those days with people planning it for weeks and weeks. We had a fair in a field near the village with hobby-horses, roundabouts, swing-boats, side-shows, those things that make the weights go up and down, and oh, all sorts of things. The men would have to climb the greasy pole and there was a prize of a leg of lamb at the top. The prizes were all practical, you know. In the afternoon we had the sports and there were potato races, egg and spoon races, sack races—all that sort of thing, and the prizes for those were joints of meat, except for the ladies who ran for two cwt of coal. Mr Medland next door would usually win a leg of lamb, mutton, or ham in one of the races. It was so funny to see all these old people going in for the different things. There were stalls out in the village, with vendors selling things; I especially remember that ice-cream—that was the highlight of the day for me, a real treat! We all used to enter things in the Flower Show, and the children would go up to the marquee in the morning to bunch wild flowers and make baskets of ferns. We would sew grasses on to cards and the best one won a prize. That had to be done in front of the committee to make sure we didn't cheat! The display was held in the school and the marquee was on the grass outside the school room. The girls and boys always did a maypole dance on the grass, and we girls wore our beautiful white voile dresses. It was fun to do that.

In the evening there was a dance held in the school room, 'cos that was the only place to hold anything like that. We were very lucky having our own band like that.

When war was declared, the Flower Show stopped. It started up again after the men came back and the war was over, but it was never the same again, you know.

The Tavistock Goosie Fair is famous internationally. In the area of Tavistock, including Buckland, children are still given a day off school to attend the fair, but in Joan's childhood it seems that many of the outlying population did not go. Probably one of the reasons was transport. The five mile journey would have been mainly walked and if one did travel by train, there was still a walk of two or three miles involved. Joan, however, suggests the fair was shunned for a very different reason:

We never went to 'Goosie Fair' as children. It was a terrible place to go—lots of drunks, a dreadful place. I don't remember going until I was walking out with Paul and then we went on his motor-bike. That was the first time ever.[13]

CHAPTER SIX

CHURCH AND THE SQUARSON

Blessid be tha pore in spurrit, vur thares es tha kindum
uv hev'n
Blessid be thay thet murn, vur that shil be
comfirtid
Blessid be tha meek, vur thay shil inhurrit tha aith
Blessid be thay which hunger an thest arter riteyissniss,
vur thay shil be vil'd
Blessid be tha macivul, vur thay shil obtayn macy,
Blessid be tha pur in hart, vur thay shil zee God,
Blessid be tha paycmeakers, vur thay shil be cal'd tha
childern a God,
Blessid be thay wich ur persecutid, vur
riteyissniss' zeake, vur thares ez tha kindum uv
hev'n.

Devon dialect version of St Matthew, Ch. five, verses 1-10 [14]

I CAN ALWAYS TELL when it is a Tuesday evening in Buckland without even looking at a newspaper or calendar, for the first clang of clapper against metal is a reminder that it is bell-ringing practice night!

Paul Bellan was for many years one of the faithful regulars who turn out, not just on Sundays, but for the midweek practice to pass on their old skills of campanology to a new generation of ringers. The weekly peal of evening bells is a fitting reminder that Joan and Paul have been life-long supporters of St Andrews Church, which stands only a matter of yards from their front door. Unfortunately Paul's ringing career, which he began when he first arrived in the village, ended abruptly shortly before his Golden Wedding anniversary in 1979. A fellow ringer committed the cardinal sin of leaving a bell 'up'. When Paul went to toll the single bell before evensong he was taken unawares and the rope yanked him off his feet. He was badly shaken and strained his arms and back.

The church itself has changed little in centuries and its treasures even include a Saxon font. Yet as far as parochial life goes 'the changes that were made since than can easily be seen'.

When Joan was a child the vicar was no short-term incumbent but reigned long and supreme over the parish in a somewhat feudal manner. Joan explained it :

Mr Haynes, the vicar, he was the squire too, because he owned the living you see, although he eventually gave it to the diocese. Can you believe it, he was here for sixty-five years? He came in 1855 and died in 1920 at the age of ninety. Reverend Baring-Gould did the same thing, and gave the living at Lewtrenchard to the Bishop of Exeter. Mr Haynes lived in the vicarage (not the house occupied by the present vicar and his family) which became the Garden House. There was a little chapel in the grounds where we used to go to Sunday-School and Bible classes, and the local Mothers' Union was started up there too. We didn't see much of Mr Haynes around the village, he was too old and tottery, but if he did come down he'd always wear his proper parson's hat you know, with the flat top and the wide

St Andrew's Church today

brim. He was a little man and he used to walk down through his fields from the vicarage. All those fields had their names. There was Vicarage Lawn, then Ten Trees (there are only eight trees now where ten limes stood, part of a whole avenue of limes between the vicarage and the Church), next came Hilly Field, Quarry Field, Second Field, and lastly Church Meadow, and those fields were kept beautiful then 'cos the gardener would have to see to them. We scrubbed the steps by the kissing gate (in between Church Meadow and Second Field) for Mr Haynes to walk over every Sunday. We didn't have to do it but we liked to and it made that blue stone look lovely. There were always cows in the fields of course, but farmers then only had two or three cows, nothing like they do now. The biggest farm then would have seven or eight. Old Mr Haynes used to chase us with a stick for swinging on the trees. There was a wall from the kissing gate and we always walked along that wall, like children do, swinging on the lime trees.

Mr and Mrs Haynes were the last people to be buried in the churchyard. Overcrowding then made it necessary for burials to be undertaken at the new cemetery, which stands opposite the new school. The Reverend L.G. Chamberlain then took over the church and a new vicarage was built on the edge of the village in 1923.

I can remember the Chamberlain family coming here. One day I was walking home from Yelverton and the church bells were ringing. When I got home my mother said:

"Mrs Northey's got another little girl."

"Oh," I said, "is that why the bells are ringing?"

'Course it turned out that a child had been born in the vicarage, their first baby. Now there's a funny thing that happened recently connected with this. My nephew came down from Bristol and at the church he goes to he told a woman that he was coming to Devon for a week.

"Oh," she said, "how lovely, I was born in Devon." Well, when he told her he was coming to Buckland Monachorum, she said: "How extraordinary, I was born in Buckland Monachorum vicarage, my father was the vicar there."

And she was the little girl I'm telling you about, the one the bells were ringing for!

Although the actual structure of the Church has changed very little, modern innovations like electricity have vastly improved the comfort for its worshippers. Joan continues:

There was no heating in the church, and for lighting we only had lamps or candles. Well, because of this we liked to go into the little Baptist Chapel (which is directly opposite Joan's cottage) on a Sunday evening. That little chapel used to be full of people you know. 'Twasn't such a big place to heat and light up. We had an afternoon service in the church as they didn't hold an evening service, especially in the winter.

There always had to be somebody going into the vestry in the church to turn a handle to work the bellows for the organ. It was somebody's job every Sunday to do that; one of the Medlands did it at one time, and I suppose they were paid a small fee for it. I would go in and 'blow' for my sister as she got older and wanted to play the organ. Well of course there was no electricity then was there?

No work was ever done on a Sunday; you know, my father wouldn't even let us sew a button on a glove! Dreadful he was, although he didn't go to church a lot. He told one of the parsons that came in one day, that it finished him when he went into church and was locked in. At the induction service of a new vicar they ring the bell, read from the lectern, preach from the pulpit, and go outside the door and lock it from the outside. That's the tradition. Well Dad had been to Rev. Streat's Induction Service and it put him off. Mr Streat had come to see why Dad hadn't been to church since and that's what he told him. Mr Streat kept on coming to see Dad, and in the end Dad said that he was doing his job and the vicar was doing his, much as to say 'you mind your busines and I'll mind mine'.

SUNDAY-SCHOOL AND EXCURSIONS

WE ALWAYS WENT to Sunday-School in the school-room and we'd come out and go into the church for the rest of the service. We sat in the aisle by the old Saxon font with Miss Bunduck, and that was the routine every Sunday, except once a month when we had a children's service in the afternoon, which we liked. The parson came out into the aisle and talked to us then.

Something that sticks out in my mind is coming out of the church one Sunday and seeing the first car in the village. It was when there were very smart people up at Pound called Champernowne and they were related to Lord Morley, I think. Well, they came down to church in this beautiful car and we little girls came out and paraded in front of it. It was so shiny and big, and we would walk round the car looking at our reflection in its shininess. At one end of the car you looked all big and at the other you'd be like a beanpole, like those funny mirrors at the fair. The Drakes came up from the Abbey in a car as well, but they'd be the only two motors out there. (Nowadays there are traffic jams outside the church as the exit from church coincides with the pub opening next door!)

Once a year we had a Sunday-School outing, and that was a steamer trip. We'd set off from Lopwell with the older children walking all the way down through Milton Combe and Lillypit, right on to Lopwell. The little children were taken in an old farm cart. And my goodness, how we dressed up! I can remember having a straw hat with a lovely big blue bow around it, and of course we had on our best dresses, special with sashes.

The steamer took us up the river to Calstock or somewhere like it, and it took all day, coming back late in the evening when it was getting dimsy (dark). We loved going up and down the stairs on the boat, down into what they called the saloon. There were nice comfortable seats down there with a table, and you could sit around and look out of the cabin windows.

Of course the outing had to be carefully planned out 'cos it always had to be when the tides were right.[15]

The steamer excursions were obviously one of the great local treats for many people, and the excitement of the occasion was apparent as Joan related to me her memories of the outings. "Until 1914 the fare to Weir Head and back—a round trip of almost forty miles—still only cost 1s. 9d." For value, comfort and enjoyment there were still no other tours in the neighbourhood to match the steamer excursions.

In their heyday these excursions saw dancing at Weir Head and on the Quay at Morwellham, while Morwell Rocks were full of picnic parties. However, young Joan and her Sunday School friends were experiencing the end of the pleasure steamer era, for as people enjoyed themselves picnicking, dancing, and to-ing and fro-ing down the river, the First World War reared its ugly head and brought a swan-song to the age of the steamer excursion. After 1914 the steamers were gradually called away to help in the war effort. After the war, although many of the steamers were either lost or too badly damaged to be used in their old role, the pageant was renewed for a short time. For two or three seasons during the 1920s the landing piers were as thronged as before the war. But the motor coach and car were now appearing as strong competitors, as Joan remembers in her account of her Sunday School outings:

Later on we got the motor vehicles and we than had 'chara-outings' when we'd all go for a trip in a

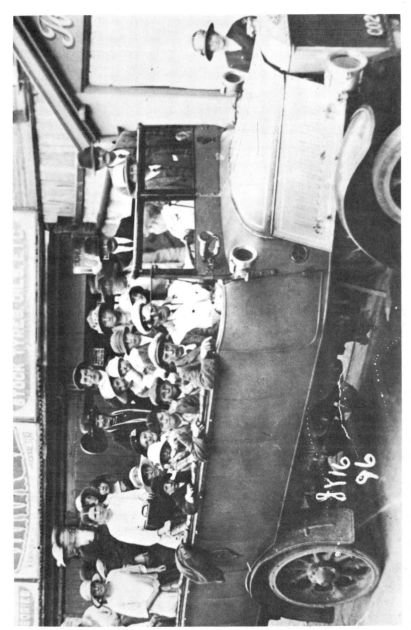

A Buckland Baptist Chapel chara-outing

charabanc. Oh, we went to many different places then; Paignton, Teignmouth, Looe . . .

The charabanc was a single decker, very high up and made out of wood. The hard wheels raised it high up off the ground and the top was open, but if it rained there was a cloth hood that could be pulled over to keep everyone dry. They were very different to the coaches now; you just can't compare can you?

In 1923 the Embankment Bus Service began to run from Plymouth to Buckland, running every day except Christmas Day. One of Joan's ex-boy-friends was an Embankment bus conductor, but she gave him up for Paul.

CHAPTER SEVEN

SHOPS AND CHARACTERS

EVERY SMALL COMMUNITY has its characters, the exceptional folk who for some reason stand out in people's memory, and Buckland Monachorum was no different. Possibly because of the prominent position they held in the local community, many of these characters were from village shops or other trades. Some stand out for traits of character, some for the events or happening to which they were unavoidably tied. Joan described some of the memorable characters of her childhood:

The first I remember about a shop is the one across the road from my cottage where Jim Fox lived. (Mr Fox was one of the village elders who had also occupied his cottage since he was a boy.) Jim Fox's parents had that house and a man called Mr Connybere and his wife Ada shared half the house with them. He had one room up and one room down and had a little room out the back where he did the cobbling. He mended all the boots and shoes in the village and his little shop window looked out onto the road and across to my cottage. It's still there now. He was a funny, surly old man and if he was in a bad mood when you went in with something to be repaired he'd throw the shoes back at you. Well, Mr Connybere and Ada had that shop which sold all sorts of stuff, groceries and the like, you know.

Another resident of the village, Mrs Rogers, also remembers going to Mr Connybere's shop as a child, taking empty jam jars to be filled with sweets. A 1 lb jar cost a farthing and a 2 lb jar cost a halfpenny. Joan went on:

Eventually Mr Connybere moved across the road to the cottage joined on to mine and rented it from Mr Pyke who was our landlord then. He used to sit by the back door and do all his cobbling but before he lived in the cottage part of it was used as the village 'Reading Room'. It belonged to the village, but there weren't any books up there that I knew of. I suppose it had been converted into the Reading Room to be used for reading, but as far as I know it was never used as that. An old man called 'Granfer' Docket used it for doing woodwork and carpentry in, and there was a wooden set of steps that he had to climb up to get to the room (later the author's bedroom!). Nobody ever used it after Old Man Docket died and eventually it was bought together with the cottage and made all one dwelling again, as it is now. Well, when Mr Connybere moved in, of course the Foxes were able to take over the rest of their cottage.

Jim Fox and his dad made all the coffins in the village and Mam would say "somebody's dead" 'cos she'd hear the hammering of the coffins, sometimes all night long. Jim was about fourteen years old when he started working for his father, and the only way they could carry their tools was on a little push trolley. It was a common sight to see them pushing their tools and wood on this heavy trolley, and of course they had to walk miles with it sometimes. As time went on Jim got a motor-bike and sidecar and of course that made things a lot easier for them. Old Granny Fox (Jim's grandmother) lived in a tiny cottage opposite the pub and she was a real old witch. If our ball went into her garden she'd never let us have it back again, she was an awful old woman. She had kept donkeys in her time and took them up on the moor for the Plymouth children to have rides on for 1d a time.

When we came here first the butcher's shop was over in Brook House (a house situated by the edge of the village brook, directly opposite the old Manor Inn) and that was where my mother's brother worked. When they gave that up as the butcher's shop, a house at the top of the hill sold meat. In fact it was the house where the terrible murder and suicide happened. That house was really the dairy, but the woman, Mrs Grepe, used to lend out the dairy on Saturday afternoons to a butcher from Horrabridge, and that's where we fetched the meat from. Of course we didn't buy that much meat from the butcher, as everyone kept a pig in their back garden. Mam'd buy a joint for the Sunday roast perhaps, 'cos we always had a roast on Sundays. I didn't like lamb then and I'll always remember my father turning the joint of lamb over and cutting 'beef' for me on the other side! For years I thought that one side was lamb and the other beef! But other than that joint it was pig meat most of the year.

Everyone in the family participated in the fattening of the pig as it was of prime importance to the family budget. A good fat pig meant a full larder and good winter and the ritual tending to poor porker is remembered here by Joan:

We'd have to buy the young pig, or slip as it was called. A slip was beyond a sucker you see, weaned off the mother pig. I can remember Dad going off to buy it from the farmer, as everyone knew when a litter had been born and the farmer let people know when the slips were

79

ready. Oh, the meat we got from those pigs when they were really fattened up . . .!

Of course all the scraps from the house went to feed the blessed pig, everything had to be saved. Even the washing up had to be done with no soap so that the water could be mixed with the meal for the pig. It was an important part of the running of the house, all the food scraps were saved and we picked dandelions from the hedgerows and fields for the pig's supper. Dad cut cartloads of ferns from the moor as bedding for it, and he was responsible for shovelling up the mess in the pig shed. Of course the pig had to have barley meal as well, and that was delivered in sacks with the flour once a fortnight. That was always a big bill to pay, and half the pig was sold to the butcher to pay for the feed. When the pig was good and fat it was time for it to be slaughtered, this was usually in December and June, 'cos we had two pigs a year. Mr Pyke always butchered the pigs when they were ready and Mam would walk as far as Ten Trees so she couldn't hear the squeals of the poor old pig. She didn't like to have anything to do with it. Mr Pyke had half-a-crown for his trouble, and after it had been slaughtered it was hung up in the back kitchen to drain for a day or two. There was no roof on that back kitchen then, only rafters, so it was nice and airy. Then Mr Pyke came back to cut it up and it was all go from then on. The bristles had to be scraped off it, and oh, the pans of boiling water that were needed! 'Course it all had to be fetched from the brook. The skin was soaked in the boiling water and then the bristles were scraped off with a scraper. It was a long, hard job and very messy. It was our job to clean out the belly and we hated doing that. The 'seltin' een' was done by Mam o' course, and we hated some of it 'cause it was too salty — 'twas horrible! But there was no deep freeze in them days so everything had to be salted. The meat was put into brine and soaked for a long time and then it was taken out and put into water to be soaked again. But when the pig had been butchered we all knew that there was plenty of meat for a while at least, and we had nice shoulder joints and hams, and of course, the hogs puddings. There would be a line of hogs puddings hanging up in the kitchen just like you see in the butcher shops.

We are undoubtedly spoiled these days by the ready and relatively cheap availability of such things as butter and cheese. We would not dream of having a slice of bread without a good spread of butter, or the modern substitute, margarine. However, Joan points out that for her butter was not always so available:

I think we got our butter from the farm and one or two of us would walk down to Fairtown (a local farm on the perimeter of the village now run as a riding stable, where butter and clotted cream are still made in the old way) once a week, usually on a Saturday morning to fetch the butter. We would sit on a bench in that scrubbed kitchen waiting for it, and the fire would be burning there, surrounded by blue-stone floor. The table was deal and was scrubbed white. Sometimes we watched them making the butter, scalding the milk and then skimming the cream from the top. It would then be worked and worked with their hands until all the water was out of it and then it was put in these moulds to set in the dairy. When the butter was taken out of the mould it would have a thistle on the top of it. They made it in 1 lb and ½ lb dabs, round and not very thick. Butter was never bought in a grocer's shop like it is now. We didn't have it very often, we had bread and jam a lot, but not butter as well, it just wasn't there to use. Jam was far more plentiful, of course, 'cos the fruit didn't cost anything to pick. Even when my mother got quite old, she wouldn't put butter and jam on bread. That would be wrong.

The farmers made their cheese as well, but it was more of a speciality, you know. We didn't have much cheese, but then we weren't a cheesey family. I've seen plenty of people making their own cream cheese out of sour milk left to hang in a muslin bag.

Some things would have to be delivered to the house as they could only be bought from some distance away. The man selling paraffin oil for the lamps would come round all the houses every Monday and of course the flour was delivered once a fortnight. It was brought in from Horrabridge from the mills there, that was where they ground it. It was strong flour and everything was made from it, cakes and bread.

The first dwelling on the right as you enter the village is the Gift House. In 1661 Sir Francis Drake, the second baronet, left £120 to build an almshouse on this spot 'for six pious persons, born and bred in the parish and none such to be put into the said house without the choice or approbation of his heir or successor'—which is to say that the lord of the manor who occupied nearby Buckland Abbey, decided just who should be allowed to live there. In 1718 another Sir Francis Drake left £5 a year for the Gift House, and it became customary to assign free rooms in the house to five elderly women, chosen by the owner of the Abbey. This was still the case when Joan was young. There was also one man, George Bailey, occupying one of the rooms.

Each room was like a little home of its own with a small iron coal range and an alcove with curtains round it for the bed. I remember Sophie Hawkins who lived there, and Mrs Brown and Mrs Stanley. On the ground floor there was one funny woman called Lizzie Jeffries who used to keep six cats for company and they were all crawling with fleas.

There was a smithy right in the village itself and the people there were called Southcott. He had his workshop next to the house and of course he was always kept very busy with all the horses around. After my children were born the smith had moved his shop to the top of the village, next to where the Women's Institute hall is now.

He had a wooden hut up there that he did all his work in, but he was a strange man called Alphonso Theophilus. He was the postman here for a time as well.

Halfway up the village street lived the Pykes, who, as I said, were our landlords for a time. Mrs Pyke had the Post Office in their house and we were quite fortunate to have a delivery every morning. The postman was called the whistling postman by everyone in the village, because he always whistled everywhere. Mr Faulkner was his real name and he was a thin little man with a big family, about eight children he had. I knew most of them as they all went to school here. Mr Pyke did the village deliveries and old Faulkner did the rest.

Mrs Pyke was stingy in her shop and we always said that when she weighed our sweets her finger was weighed in with them. There wasn't one too many.[16] She was a big tall woman who played whist a lot, and she used to win all the prizes, but if for some reason she didn't win it was a different job! He was a nice old man and quite a landowner in these parts. He owned the present playing fields and kept chickens there. He also rented another field in the village and cut it for hay every year to feed his pony. He was somebody of importance in the village as he also had the only conveyance, the pony and jingle. The jingle was a trap, you know, all open with seats around it for you to sit on. He had a dog called Nigger which was a black and tan mongrel and our dog Toby hated him. Every time Nigger Pyke passed the door Toby barked and barked.

In this little cottage on the corner (opposite Joan's cottage and next door to Jim Fox's, and owned by him and his parents before him) there lived a man and his sister called Bill and Sophie Hawkins. We children always tantalised them because Sophie was so nosey. They'd be having their tea and if something or somebody different came into the village she'd be out and she'd go right across the road with her tea cup in her hand to throw away the dregs. And if anybody came to our house she'd be up at that window looking in to see who it was. There was nothing else to do but to be nosey. So this old Bill Hawkins, every time leap-year came around we girls would propose to him, and oh, such fun we had. He was such a funny old fat man you know. My father used to cut his hair for him out in our back garden, and he came up one Saturday when my Dad had had a drink more than he ought 'ave had; p'raps he'd been drinking his cider, any rate Dad nipped his ear, and old Bill, he said :

"Bugger to Hell Tom Kelloway, you've nipped my bloody ear!" And he was only half cut but he ran out that back gate home.

There were a lot of the old roadsters about when I was a child, and there was one in particular who came to our house a lot. Mam called him Figgy Blowey. He came in once with three starlings; I think he'd knocked them on the head or something; and he asked Mam to make them into a pie. We children called it 'starvin' pie', he must have been starving to eat it! He always wore an awful battered bowler hat and those britches and leggins like my dad's, only 'course they were really tatty. He often came in to see us 'cos Mam made him a cup of tea and he was a good old man, everybody liked him. Figgy didn't go to a workhouse like most of the roadsters who just passed from one workhouse to the other, stopping at houses on the way to ask for some hot water to make their tea. No, Figgy came from a good family—Blowey's who farmed here for years, but he was sort of an outcast. He lived rough under the hedges, anywhere he could find. I don't know where he got his food from, 'cos there wasn't any money, was there? P'raps he did casual work on a farm, but he shouldn't have been as he was, that Blowey, coming from such a good family.

There was always gipsies at the top of the village, not living in caravans but in huts. They must have put them up when they arrived 'cos they stayed for some time, you know. I can remember going to school with the gipsy children. They were supposed to have been a thieving lot and, of course, they often poached for rabbit. The women sold pegs round and about but they weren't pegs like we know them now, they were just bits of wood tied at the top. Our gipsy men were dressed very colourfully with bright handkerchiefs round their necks and the women wore them around their hats.

Today it is recognised by education authorities and social service departments alike that truancy is a real problem, sometimes culminating in the parents of the offender appearing before a court. Joan's childhood days were no different, as she now recalls:

The kid-catcher was a man I well remember. We called him that because he came to the school as the attendance officer to catch the children who played truant. His real name was Billy Beer and my goodness, if children didn't go to school then he'd know the reason why. Parents were afraid not to send their children to school because they'd have to pay a heavy fine. Billy Beer lived in the village with his sister who was deaf (her job was to clean the church).

Billy married Miss Browning our Sunday School teacher, and her parents were very much against the marriage, although she was by then a woman of forty. Well, she was married quietly one wet Sunday morning with only her sister attending the wedding. My mother had got wind that she was being married, and was there to welcome her when she came out of the church. Miss Browning told me how delighted she was:

"The first one I saw on the church steps was your mother, Joan."

Not even her parents were at the wedding. They had a boot business in Plymouth and I suppose they wanted her to carry on helping them. Anyway we adored them as a couple, in fact she's the one I started doing drama with when I was about eighteen.

The people who kept the Drake Manor Inn were called Stevenson, and they had a blind son called Dennis. He was our church organist and he was marvellous when he played it. He always wore dark black glasses. His mother was a very smart woman with jet black hair; she was always so well dressed and presented. Mr Stevenson was a little man whose sister was the teacher in the infants' class of the school.

In such a tight-knit community everybody knew their neighbours' business, but dwellings situated on the more isolated outskirts of the village held a few secrets. For example, the genealogy of some inhabits was a bit of a mystery, and the family produced by a certain military gentleman was a subject of whispered gossip. Joan, anxious not to embarrass or offend those still living, nevertheless explained, withholding the real names:

There was this gentleman, called himself Captain, and when we were children my brother Alf would take the milk to his cottage for an extra penny or two. Well one day when Alf was there he saw a girl. No-one knew there were any children living there and there was a great big hedge all around the house, so he asked this Captain who the girl was. He told Alf that she was a dead soldier's child, but really they were his, you see! He kept them hid away in that cottage, four of them: two boys and two girls. This Captain lived there and he had a housekeeper who people said was the children's mother. I don't suppose many have found out the secret because if Alf hadn't been taking the milk there he wouldn't have found out either, would he? He kept hearing these children's voices but could never see them until the day he saw this girl. That dead soldier weren't so dead!

THE TERRIBLE SHOOTINGS

MOST OF THE VILLAGE CHARACTERS are remembered for fairly trivial happenings and idiosyncratic details that tend to stick in one's memory, but there was one more than vivid incident in the village that shook everyone. It was a violent event, involving a family who were friends of many in the community.[17]

Joan had a vivid recollection:

We were playing in Butt Park (a field which has since been built on, then outside the village) when someone came running to say that Bill Combes had murdered his sister Beatie Grepe and had killed himself with a shotgun at their home. (They lived at No. 1 The Village, next to the Gift or Alms House, in the cottage which was the dairy.) Beatie was actually his step-sister and was a lot younger than him. He was thirty-one and she was eighteen, and he was in love with her. I've a feeling that he was jealous 'cos she had a young man she was walking out with and he's supposed to have said:

"If I can't have you than nobody else shall!"

Anyway he borrowed this shotgun to shoot rabbits he said, and then went home with it. Apparently he called up the stairs:

"Beatie, the butcher's here, come down."

And as she came down the stone steps—it was a spiral stone staircase leading into the sitting-room—he shot her. His older step-sister Annie was out in the back kitchen and she heard the shot:

"What's that Bill?" she said.

"Come in and see," he replied, and then she heard another shot and went in. She found her sister dead on the stairs, and he had blown his brains out.

The village was so terribly upset; the reaction was dreadful because we all loved Beatie so much. She was like our Maid Marion, so lovely to all the children that used to flock round her. You'd always see her with the children around her while she sat in the porch of her cottage crocheting or knitting. We made a real heroine of her, you know, like children do with somebody older.

The dreadful incident was even more tragic since Mr Grepe had been killed three years earlier in a wagoning accident while crossing Dartmoor, and Mrs Grepe, the mother, was awaiting an operation in

No. 1, The Village

hospital at the time of the shooting. Joan told me of a strange premonition that the old woman had had on the day of the killing:

She knew all this was happening because she'd had a dream in hospital. Annie, her daughter, went to visit her mother on the Sunday afternoon following the shootings, and she told Annie about this dream.

"What's the matter?" said Mrs Grepe. "What's Bill done?"

"Bill done, why?" said Annie.

Mrs Grepe: "Oh, there's something awful going to happen, if it hasn't happened, it's going to."

Of course Annie thought this was extraordinary when her mother asked what Bill was doing and if he and Beatie were all right. Well, Annie had to lie, poor soul. She had to say, yes, they were all right. But how dreadful it was for that poor girl, to go in and see her mother in hospital and keep such a dreadful thing from her, when all the time she'd had this dream.

The mother was told the full details of the tragedy some days later.[18]

John was buried at 11 am after a service in the Baptist Chapel. The interment of Beatrice took place in the afternoon. Joan said:

I'll always remember my father and mother telling us they'd buried him right over by the hedge in the cemetery; and her grave is about ten yards away.

The identical tombstones can still be seen:
In Loving Memory of John Combes
Beloved son of H. and A. Grepe
Died July 26th 1913 Aged 31
Thy Will Be Done
and the same for Beatrice except the inscription at the bottom:
In Loving Memory of Beatrice Grepe
Beloved daughter of H. and A. Grepe
Died July 26th 1913 Aged 18
Gone but not forgotten

CHAPTER EIGHT

"NEAREST TO SCHOOL
AND LATEST TO GET THERE"

TODAY WE ARE CONSTANTLY encouraged to take an interest in the education of our children. Many schools have lively parent-teacher associations and all have open days to which parents are invited. We are made aware of new ideas in education and of the need to encourage the child and stimulate his interest in a wide spectrum of subjects. There remain few single-sex schools and nowadays boys and girls alike can enjoy such things as woodwork, cookery, technical drawing and needlework. Life in the classroom is a free, pleasant experience with none of the rigid discipline enforced on pupils like Joan some seventy years ago. Schooling for her meant, being taught the basic three 'R's, reading, writing and arithmetic, singing and sewing.

There wasn't all the fancy equipment schools have now. I can remember having to use meat skewers as knitting needles. We did a lot of sewing at school, making our aprons and chemises, but I don't think we ever wore the chemise. The sewing was beautiful then you know, everything had to be perfect. The chemise had embroidery around the neck and armholes and had tiny little gathers that we had to stroke with a needle to get them to lie properly. It took such a long time because it was all done by hand, we didn't have things like sewing machines at school then. I can particularly remember having to strike these gathers as Mrs Baker our headmistress was so fussy about sewing. We made all these aprons and chemises out of calico and when we had finished them we could take them home with us.[19]

It took perhaps a term to make a chemise and that was our sewing lesson, you see. Mrs Baker taught us tapestry work as well and we did all sorts of things like that and I can well remember having a square and doing a nice little design of a pansy, little samplers and the sort. We took weeks and weeks to finish our work, such care went into it all. I don't see them do anything like it now. Sewing, drawing, and singing were important in the school, and oh, the singing we did! Mrs Baker always made us sing and we had end of term concerts when our parents came in to hear us. We sang songs like 'The Minstrel Boy' ('The minstrel boy to the wars has gone,') 'Flag of Britain Proudly Waving' and 'The Hyacinth' which went like this:

Oh beautiful hyacinth cousin*
The sweetest wildflower that grows
How graceful you stand on your sturdy green stems
To me you're sweet as a rose.

* the bluebell

91

I always think of that song when the bluebells are out. We sang a song about the peas in your garden which went like this:

Nine little prisoners shut in a shell
Grew in a garden fair, close by a well
Nine bonny babies tucked in so tight
Tired of darkness, longing for light.

We performed plays at school, as well, for the end of term, and I can remember doing 'Goody Two Shoes' very well one Christmas time. A special platform was erected in the school for us to do the play on, and for the concerts.

Mr Baker was the headmaster, but we all called him Maista. Of course the boys' and girls' schools were separate, so Mr Baker taught the boys in the bottom school, helped by Miss Crossman, while Mrs Baker, Miss Wootten and Miss Stevenson taught the girls. We had two rooms in the girls' school, the infants in one room with Miss Stevenson, and two classes in the other room. School started at nine in the morning and finished at four in the afternoon, and I can well remember putting our boots on in the morning, struggling 'cos of the chilblains on our feet, and Mam shouting at us:

"Nearest to school and latest to get there !"

It would take us so long to get these boots on us you know. Of course we came home to have our lunch because we were so close, although most of the children had to bring a pasty or sandwiches to school. They put their pasties round the big black stove in the classroom to keep them warm and the smell was lovely, made you feel quite hungry!

The school was what was called an elementary school and I didn't ever go in the infants' room as I was over the age of seven when we moved to Buckland. But my little sister Barbara was in the infants' class and she had

Miss Stevenson, who was a very fussy woman. She didn't think anything of clipping the children across the head. I was awfully timid, and once when I was in my line Miss Stevenson clipped Alf (my brother) across the ear for something he'd done and he hadn't been at school very long. Well Barbara stepped out of her line and said:

"My mother says if you clip Alf again, she'll come and clip you."

Of course she was punished for that, for speaking out.

My teacher was Miss Wootten and we liked her, although she was a bit crotchety and very strict, but they all were then. She was a very tall, angular woman, with a knob of hair that sat on top of her head. I think the teacher we liked the best was Mrs Baker, but she was also stern, and we'd get six of the best across our hands if we did anything wrong, especially if she saw us talking in class. Mr Baker put the boys across his knee when he gave 'em the stick, but the boys had the notion that if they put a horse hair across their backsides, it broke the cane. I don't know if it ever did.

Mrs Baker was very annoyed with me once because I put up my hand and asked to be moved to a different place in the class. Well, when she asked me why, I said:

"'Cos there's fleas crawling all over Fanny Walter's face."

And they were, they were crawling all over her! Well, we all had long hair to our waists, and it was an awful time for fleas and lice in those days. Mrs Baker wouldn't let me move, but I went as far as I could away from Fanny. Mrs Baker didn't like you to get the first word in; children spoke when they were spoken to. We were brought up in a very Victorian way, nothing like today.

Our lessons at school were very basic and down to earth; reading, writing and arithmetic—the three 'R's; there never seemed to be a minute wasted. A regular period was our drill or physical education, as it's known now, and if the weather was right it was held outside, if not, inside. Of course we had no other clothes to change into like they do now; it all had to be done in the clothes we went to school in, but the drill itself was very formal and we all had to do the exercises in time with each other . . . 'one, two, three, four', that sort of thing.

On Friday afternoons we had one period of silent reading when we could choose the book we wanted to read and carry on with it each week, and we didn't dare talk to each other 'else we got a rap across the knuckles with the ruler. I particularly liked that lesson when I remember reading my favourite book, 'A Peep Behind the Scenes'—I could read it again now if I had it. Handwriting was taught at school from a very early age. I sent my mother a postcard from Torquay when I was only about six and it was lovely writing, not like they do now, but 'twas in double, joined-up writing. The pens were wooden handled and we'd have to dip them in the ink. It was pot luck as to whether you got a good nib or not, sometimes they were cross-pointed and then you'd have to go out and ask for another one, sometimes they'd be coarse and sometimes fine.

We did a bit of geography and history and I think out of the two I preferred geography. I learnt about the Empire, standing around a big globe in the classroom, and was told of all the different countries then; they all belonged to someone didn't they? (In Joan's childhood a large part of any atlas or globe was coloured pink, the colour symbolising the countries belonging to the great British Empire, the largest empire since the days of the Romans.)

I'm not boasting, but I was actually very good at school, and I passed the exam for pupil-teaching which would have meant me going to Tavistock Grammar School. But Mam and Dad couldn't afford to let me go because although it was a scholarship, all the books had

94

to be bought and there were a lot of other expenses. There was another boy who passed, the same age as me, called Percy Voaden, but he was an only child, and he went to Tavistock to become a pupil-teacher. He had to walk to and fro every day. Anyway I couldn't go so I stayed on in Standard VII, which was the top one at this school, until I was fourteen.

THE GREAT WAR

WHEN I WAS STILL at school the fighting hadn't begun and we didn't hear anything at all about war. The First World War changed all that. I was about eleven years old when it began . . .

When I look today at this sleepy village it seems incredible that its inhabitants should have been involved in not one but two horrific wars. Flanders Fields and those many other now infamous grave-yards seem a world away, but it was in such tiny communities as Buckland that the war took its worst toll and changed the whole way of life. Part of a generation died young, and with it went the old ways. Even those who survived the carnage in one piece, besides those who came home again with dreadful injuries, could not look at the world around them in quite the same way as they had viewed it in the bucolic days before the conflict. Joan's father was one of many who never actually 'went over the top' but he suffered terribly ever after as a result of his own war effort:

He went into the Yeomanry because they worked with horses and there weren't much he didn't know about them. They sent him to Bridgend in Wales to train Canadian horses for the front. He wasn't in the actual fighting line but had an awful accident with one of the horses when he was thrown, crushing his head. He'd only been away about two years. In hospital the doctors never thought he'd survive but he pulled through and came home an invalid. He wasn't right after that. Years later a lot of fluid drained down to his ribs and he had to have two of them removed. He had to wear a spinal jacket for years, all because of that war and he was one of the lucky ones!

When he got a bit better after recovering from his injuries he was able to do light jobs like looking after the cemetery and gardening. He got a disability pension too, and the funny thing is that during the war we were better off as a family because the army gave an allowance for each child.

Even the Buckland children were expected to contribute to the war effort, led by Miss Beer the Bible Class teacher.

During the war we all went once a week up to the Gift House where Miss Beer would give out the wool for the Red Cross knitting in a room at the back of the house. We often went down to Grenofen—a walk of more than two miles—to collect spagnum to fill pillows for the wounded soldiers coming back from the war. Mam would dry it on the stove after we had carried it back home and the moss made pillows lovely and soft. I believe Mam made shirts for the soldiers as well.

Miss Beer was an enormous woman who would look over the top of her glasses at us as she taught us to say special prayers for peace:

Give peace in our time, oh Lord,
Because there is none other that fighteth for us
But only Thou oh Lord.

A lot of men and boys went to fight in the war, boys we knew who were only eighteen years old, and they became sailors as well as soldiers. Jack Medland next door went, Jack Moor and Harry Bowie . . . they were all the same age group, you see. I remember one man from the village who died. He was a sailor, but he wasn't killed in action, just died of measles on board his ship. His wife was four months pregnant at the time so the baby was born not knowing her father. We saw the

Zeppelins in the sky but they didn't do any harm here. We heard all about them of course and about mines at sea and the submarine threat.

By the time the 1914-1918 war ended Joan was no longer a schoolgirl but a servant-girl in one of the local big houses:

I was in service at Yelverton on Armistice Day and I well remember the celebrations. It was a very wet afternoon which spoiled it a bit, but everyone was so thrilled about the war being over, it didn't make much difference. There was a big marquee up on the moor at Yelverton and the Buckland band made the music. We had sports and there were hooters going all afternoon. The noise was quite overwhelming. There was special tea in the marquee and I had the children in my charge with me. Medals were presented to the men who had come home from the war, including my father, and that was a very proud moment for us. In the evening a bonfire was lit and everyone sang all the old war songs round the fire.

IN SERVICE

THESE DAYS it is difficult to imagine a young girl going into 'service', for teenage girls have opportunities on leaving school that their grandmothers could not have imagined. Their earning power is far higher and their status in a competitive world is much improved, with school-leavers being able to benefit from holidays, good working conditions and regular hours; to say nothing of the choice they have before them on leaving school. College or university entrance no longer depends totally upon whether one's parents can afford the fees and expenses and a modern girl can choose a career once exclusively for men. Joan's childhood days were different, for the only opportunity open to a girl on leaving school was to do all the menial tasks in somebody else's house for next to nothing.[20] For all that, these jobs were highly sought after and prized, for girls like Joan were expected to help out with the family budget:

97

I was fourteen years old when I went out to work for my first family. They lived up near Yelverton which was too far to walk every day so of course I had to live in. I went as the nursery maid for sixteen shillings a month, but I was really miserable there and cried and cried to come home. I was allowed home once a fortnight but that was all and then I'd be allowed home for church in the morning but I'd have to be back in the house again at lunchtime (and it was a walk of two miles each way). Then if I came out in the afternoon I'd have to be back by seven in the evening. We were allowed very little time to ourselves, it was mostly work you know.

I'd have to get up and prepare the childrens' breakfast (there were two children—a boy of six and a girl of four)—and then get them ready for their governess. The night nursery was next, and that had to be cleaned right through and the beds made. The lady of the house would then set me various jobs to do for her, as I was supposed to be a sort of lady's maid as well. There was always sewing to do and I can remember having to brush her hair a lot.

Some of the housework was back-breaking, 'cos we didn't have any appliances like carpet sweepers. Cleaning the carpets was a big job that we did about once a fortnight. Mind you, we had some ingenious ideas for doing it even without all these modern gadgets.

We used to put newspaper in buckets of water until they were damp; that would keep the dust down. After putting the newspaper all over the floor we'd brush with a hard bristle brush and get all the dust up. The damp paper kept the dust down. Another method was to sprinkle well-washed and strained tea-leaves everywhere and then brush them up.

Spring cleaning was a job too. That was the only time the servant staff were given an egg to eat. Eggs were not eaten like they are now. We were lucky to have one mixed up in a pan and divided between three of us. We were only allowed a whole egg each at Easter. Normally for our midday meal we had something light and cooked and then just bread and cake for tea. We used to be given saffron cake, which we nicknamed 'hungry cake' because there was hardly anything in it. But the egg was the big treat, one each after spring cleaning.

In the afternoon it was my job to amuse the children, so I'd usually end up taking them for walks until tea-time. Then I'd get their tea, and the governess's tea and take the children down to see their mother for half an hour or so before they went to bed. It was a very long day for a fourteen-year-old.

Well, when I'd finished for the day I went down into the kitchen for my supper. It was more cosy down there with all the others on the staff, and we used to chat round the table long after supper had finished. But this lady always made me go to bed by nine o'clock because I was so young. I shared a bedroom with the cook who I'll always remember because she had a funny name, Ephra. It was a nice room divided down the middle by a screen, but it was unusual because she was the oldest servant in the house and I was the youngest, and somehow we ended up sharing.

I didn't like the lady of the house at all. One particular Sunday when we were all sitting round the table in the kitchen having our supper, this lady swept through and said:

"Stand up Joan as I walk through."

She only said it to me, although everyone else was sitting down as well. She picked on me to make me have manners I suppose, but it's something I've never forgotten. That's how they treated you. I think this lady did like me, but she wanted to rule me all the time. She would give me all sorts of little presents and clothes because she'd like to dress me up. I can remember once I went up to my room and on the dressing table there was a pot of face cream and I thought this was a gift from her so I put some on. Well, when I next saw her she asked me if I'd seen this pot of cream because she'd lost it and I knew then that she'd been looking through my room and had left her cream there by mistake.

It is well known that 'Upstairs, Downstairs' staff were subject to unscrupulous employers but most were too afraid to complain. Not Joan . . .

Her husband was horrible as well, and although he was a military gentleman, I thought he was a lecherous old man. I knew he chased Lily the parlour maid around, and she had to lock herself in her bedroom to get away from him. He'd give that Lily boxes of chocolates and all sorts of things, and she would come down into the kitchen and share them with us all. But I was younger and when he started on me I was frightened. If he saw me be bending down, brushing up or something, I'd suddenly feel him running his fingers up my back. So it went on until one day I was up on the back landing in what they called the housemaids' cupboard (a large walk-in cupboard) and he came up the back stairs. I looked out of the cupboard to see who it was and when he saw me there he started going like this (kiss, kiss) at me. When he got to the door I said :
"If you dare to touch me I shall go straight to your wife".

I can see his face now, he just bowed his head at me and went right on downstairs. He never tried it on again, but you see he'd fancy any young girl, I think. I was so young and he frightened me to death, really shaking I was. In the end I told Mam and Dad about it on one of my visits home and they took me away. But that's what used to happen in some of those houses.

From there I went to Huckworthy as the under-nurse. The family there was lovely and they had three young children, one of whom I well remember because when he grew up he became the master of one of the local hunts. Mike was his name, and I've told him since when there was a meet in the village how I used to have to lift him onto the toilet when he was only about three years old! I was ever so happy at that house and stayed there for about three years, but it was still so far from home. My father would have to walk to Horrabridge and there was a woodman who lived near the house at Huck-worthy who would take me the rest of the way. This woodman would come down to the pub at Horrabridge and I suppose Father would call in and have a drink, and then I'd walk on up the rest of the way with the woodman. The family I was working for were hunting people and I remember that they kept lots of horses and hounds. Well, then a Colonel and Mrs Johnson moved to Yelverton and they wanted a house-parlour maid and as it was so far to walk to Huckworthy, I went there. It was strange because they had bought the house that my first employers lived in, the ones I didn't like, but the Johnsons were a dear couple with two grown-up daughters. One, Jean, worked for a church in Devonport, and the other, Elsie, lived at home. But you know you still weren't expected to ask for a night off to go to a dance or a social; they didn't expect you to ask and it was considered dreadful if you did. Barbara by then was in service with a Lady Harris at The Brake and these old ladies like Lady Harris would have what they called 'at home' days. This was a particular day each week when they were at home to any-one who wanted to call for tea. Mrs Johnson would tell me after she'd been to one of these at homes that Lady Harris would say:

"I wish you wouldn't let Joan go to these dances, because when she wants to go to a dance Barbara wants to go to a dance and I've got to let her off."

We'd only ask for a night off; we had to be back by the next morning.

Generally you were only allowed your evening off, and then you had to be back by nine or half-past. I was working for the Johnsons when I met Paul and I've been outside that door saying goodnight to him when the door's been banged because I haven't been in on time. They'd make me ring the bill and I'd have a jawin' when I got inside.

But the old Colonel was a dear old man, and he never settled down in his bed till he knew I was in safely. I'd always have to go in and say goodnight to him, and one evening he said to me:

"Remember Joan when the old man's gone, you've been as dear as a daughter to him."

That's what made it so painful for me when he died. He was an invalid and he went away to have some drastic treatment on his arthritic hip, but they say his heart never stood the strain. He died suddenly up on the moor. He'd gone to see his daughter Jean off on the bus to go back to Plymouth, and when they got to the top of the moor he dropped. Jean came running back:

"Quick, Joan, the Colonel's fallen."

I ran out and we called somebody off the moor to help us carry him in. I can remember rushing around getting him towels and hot bottles and we laid him on the chesterfield in the dining room. But he was dead, you know, but I became ill, the doctor said I had an ulcer through the shock and strain of it all. I was really ill and eventually had to come home, where I stayed for six months.

The Johnsons often came down to ask when I was coming back, but I didn't feel I could go back to that house. I went to look after two little boys in Yelverton then, but only for a short time because by then I was engaged to be married to Paul.

102

My brother introduced me to Paul who moved here from Sydenham Damerel, that's right over the other side of Lamerton. His parents had a smallholding there, but his mother got very ill and they had to break up the home. His mother had rheumatoid arthritis and went to a sister in Plymouth to be cared for, and of course Paul's father went as well. Paul took a farm job in Tamerton Foliot and he was in lodgings with the farmer when they moved here, so he came with them. I was about twenty-one when I met him and he had a BSA motor-bike. That was a big thing then you know; everyone thought he was well off! And he had the nickname of Hellfire Jack. I was going with Paul for three years before we got married. We had to save, you see, which is why I had to go back to work after I was ill, to earn some money. I don't think we saw much of our wages 'cos they had to help out Mam and Dad at home. Girls won't go into service now. They wouldn't put up with it.

Hellfire Jack on his motor-bike

CHAPTER NINE

THEN . . . AND . . . NOW

ON AUGUST 14th in the summer of 1979, the whole of Buckland Monachorum joined in the celebration of Joan and Paul Bellan's golden wedding anniversary. The festivities centred on Rose Cottage . . . the same home where Joan's parents had celebrated their 50 years of marriage. Overwhelmed by a mountain of presents, a flurry of cards that weighed down the postman for several mornings' deliveries, and what seemed like a complete nursery's stock of flowers, Joan sat down one evening with me to reflect on her married life.

"It seems like yesterday," she said, thumbing through her fading wedding album photos of 1929.

She was twenty-six years old and Paul twenty-seven when they married and first lived at Summerleaze, Yelverton, a tithe cottage that went with Paul's job as a gardener.

Their first son, Eric was born a year later, and because the chimney smoked so badly the family moved and occupied several

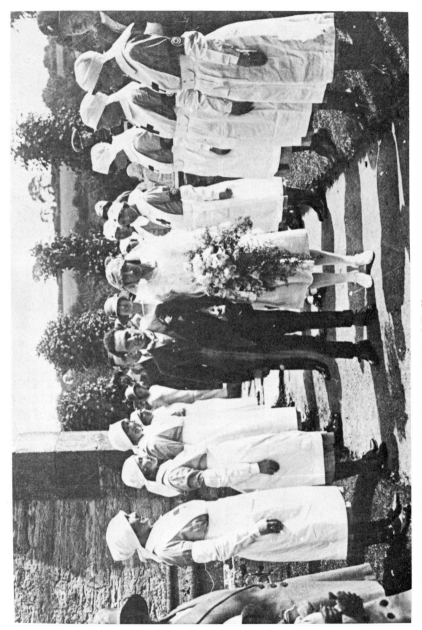

A Red Cross guard of honour for Joan and Paul Bellan

houses in and around Buckland until they finally settled in Arranmore, a house on the outskirts, in 1939. By this time, another son, Ian, had arrived and Joan was bringing up her young family under much the same conditions as her mother but with the added difficulties of wartime. She had no running water, just a hand pump in the kitchen which had a nasty habit of drying up every summer just when it was needed most. Then the water had to be fetched from the nearby stream. There was no electricity, so oil lamps were the only source of light.

The family had a bath . . . but no taps!

The water had to be fetched in buckets and heated up on the copper just like my Mam had to do it. I think we lost out on that really, because we couldn't have our nice new bath in front of the fire like we did before with the old tin tub.

(In one respect Joan was even worse off than her mother): My copper was outside so I had to go out in the cold to do the washing whereas me Mam's was in the back kitchen.

When Joan and Paul took over Arranmore they also inherited 400 hens and ran it as a poultry farm. Joan recalls the early days of this venture:

We were there for six months before we even picked up a single egg from the bloomin' things. We could only get nine pence a dozen for eggs and two shillings and sixpence for each hen, so we used to kill off just a few at a time and sell them at Plymouth market.

Things were so tight; Paul was anxious to join the Royal Air Force but his skill on the land was recognised as being of more value to the country in its time of need, so he broke up some hard ground and managed to coax even more badly needed vegetables out of the soil to ease the wartime shortage of food.

At the outbreak of the Second World War Paul had also turned one of the hen houses over to rabbit production and these too were butchered for their meat—something Joan was not too keen on:

I found this hard to accept 'cos I'm a bit of a softie really. I would never eat any of our rabbits. Silly isn't it?

107

I was daft, 'cos if any of the young rabbits or chicks were born weak I'd have them in the house and keep them warm in the kitchen and hand feed 'em . . . only for them to be butchered later on.

During their fifteen years at Arranmore, their daughter Pauline was born, and then the family moved to Whitehall, a lovely cottage in the village belonging to a farmer, Stan Ward. The garden was overgrown and unmanageable until Paul got stuck in, and within the first year won the prize for the best kept garden in Yelverton and Buckland.

When Joan's mother died in 1963 they moved back into her childhood home, after buying the rest of the family's share in Rose Cottage. Joan had come full circle in her lifetime. The simple daughter of serving parents, a servant-girl herself, with the barest education, is a proud grandmother to six grandchildren, among them a talented young violinist who won a place in the famous National Youth Orchestra and a chorister in the Exeter Cathedral Choir. So does she think children have got everything too easy these days?

Well, they've got so much laid on for them like television and radio. The new swimming-pool at the school is another example; it must make life easier for them and more pleasant. But then I don't remember any lay-abouts in my day, the parents just wouldn't allow it. P'raps it's the fault of parents and not the children now. There was far more discipline and strictness. My father always used to warn me:

"I'll cut your legs off if you bring any trouble home here."

I think everyone did far more together as a family then as well. Like every Sunday evening, after tea and Bible Class we were taken up over the moors for a walk. My Dad would pick branches out of the hedgerows and make us a little whistle each. He'd get the bark off, make a little hole and then slip the skin back on again. It was a lovely little toy. How many parents have got the time to do that sort of thing nowadays? Mind you, fathers were around more then to eat and play with their family because they worked locally and didn't have to commute to jobs like they do today.

... 'The changes that were made since then can easily be seen ...' goes the song, and Joan thinks that it is the case, as far as women are concerned.

There's no doubt about it, I think wives and mothers today have got it much easier. Everything's there for them at the touch of a button ... it gives you time to do so many other things. Every waking hour was spent in the home looking after your family's needs. There were no opportunities to work elsewhere or do anything else.

Certainly Joan's generation was one of the last to practise the dying art of being happy on little. Were they, then, the good old days? She mused:

You know, it's hard to say. I do wish we'd had some of the gadgets and luxuries when I was young, but somehow we were more satisfied doing things the hard way. They say, 'what you don't have, you don't miss'—it's difficult to see what we've missed.

There's plenty of things, good and bad, we've experienced, that tomorrow's children will never know about. But them days have gone, and that's that.

Rose Cottage and the Author's home

The Inn — now the Drake Manor

NOTES AND BIBLIOGRAPHY

Chapter 1

Note

1 *Muckram Wakes*—Derbyshire Folk Group (Leader Records, available from Cecil Sharp House, London) includes song, '50 Years Ago'.

2 *Sabine Baring-Gould—Squarson, Writer and. Folklorist* by Bickford H. Dickinson (David and Charles, Newton Abbot, Devon).

3 *Horrabridge Village Book* (Horrabridge Pensioners' Club, available from Horrabridge shops.)

Chapter 4

4 *My Dartmoor* by Clive Gunnell (Bossiney Books, St Teath, Cornwall) tells of another Dartmoor character with the inherited gift of charming, who could only pass it on to a female relative.

5 *Life in a Devon Village* by Henry Williamson (Faber and Faber, 1944) refers to charmers as 'white witches' and lists a few charms. The following was a copy of a white witch's incantation 'with the authentic spelling, handed down during how many centuries,' for curing something known as white swelling: As our Blessed Lord can cure all manar of diseases, of a white ill thing, a red ill thing, a black ill thing, a rotted ill thing, an haking ill thing, a cold clapping ill thing, a hot preaking (ill thing), a bizzing ill thing, a sticking ill thing, let all drop from thy face, thy head, thy fleash unto the earth in the name of the Father, Son and Holy Ghost, Amen.

Another mentioned was for 'stenten' or staunching bleeding . . . As our Blessed Lord and Saviour went down into River Jordan to be baptized and the water was vile and hard, our Lord Jesus was mild and good he laid his hand and it stood so, and so shall thy Issue of thy blood . . . In the name of the Father, Son and Holy Ghost, Amen.

Nummits and Crummits—Devon Customs, Characteristics and Folklore by Sarah Hewitt (reprinted E.P. Publishing Ltd, Wakefield, first published 1900), gives the following examples:

To remove warts

Take an eel and cut off the head
Rub the warts with the blood off the head
Then bury the head in the ground
When the head is rotted the warts fall off.

To heal burns

The witch repeats the following prayer while passing her hands three times over the burn

Three wise men came from the East
One brought fire, two carried frost

Out fire! Out frost!
In the name of the Father, Son and Holy Ghost.

The book also reveals cures for the colic, charms for toothache and staunching blood, fever and 'zweemy-headedness' where one would have to 'wash the head with plenty of old rum. The back and face with sour wine; wear flannel next to the skin, and carry a packet of salt in the left-hand pocket.'

The Hedgerow Book by Ron Wilson (David and Charles) tells of a Cornish custom when 'seven bramble leaves were picked and purified in spring water, then placed on any inflamation or swelling;' and the following was repeated three times for each of the seven leaves (a very similar charm to the one above):

There came three angels from the East
One brought fire and two brought frost
Out fire and in frost,
In the name of the Father, Son and Holy Ghost.

6 *The Witchcraft and Folklore of Devon* by Ruth St Leger-Gordon (Robert Hale, Ltd 1965), says it is curious that the Dartmoor pixie is often confused with the natural will-o'-the-wisp *ignis fatuus*. The weird lights, also known as Jack-o'-lanterns, seen flickering on lonely parts of the moor may account for old beliefs about the little people. This natural phenomenon is rarely seen, but another village elder, Bill Northmore, in *Outreach*, the Buckland Monachorum Parish Magazine, wrote a description of it:

We lived in Shadycombe . . . in 1914 while there, I saw for the first and only time a will-o'-the-wisp become airborne. Under certain conditions bogs or mires give off an inflammable gas. On occasions the gases become ignited and can be seen bobbing along the surface of the mire. It is very unusual for these gases to be carried along on the breeze. However that is just what I saw.

I remained glued to the ground while this phenomenon passed overhead making a swishing sound and changing shape constantly—like something of out Dr Who. Being only about nine years of age at the time I was, of course, very scared, but after finding out the cause it was an experience I would not have missed.

Mr Northmore was a village bellringer for fifty-one years and Vicar's warden for twenty.

Seamus Ennis—Master Piper and Tale Teller (Leader Records, includes pixie-led stories and tunes) records a very good example—told in inimitable Irish style—by the great uillean piper, Seamus Ennis. He says that old people will tell you to reverse your coat whenever you get lost, to overcome the pixie spell. This charming little folk tale is then followed by 'The Fairie's Hornpipe'.

7   *Buckland Monachorum* (Booklet by Buckland Monachorum Women's Institute, 1930s, available from some local sources). This is indeed a general superstition, which anyone who studies folklore will often come across.

8   Another villager, born and bred, Mrs Margaret Rogers, told me of an old man she knew who was a resident at a local nursing home in which she worked. She stripped back the sheets of his bed to make it and found to her surprise several corks. She asked him why they were in his bed and he showed her the top of his leg, around which was tied a string of corks, threaded onto elastic. He wore them to help his rheumatoid arthritis.

   Another old woman known to Mrs Rogers asked her to find her three corks, as she had four, but needed another three to make the seven go round her leg.

   Mrs Rogers also remembered being told of people who warmed salt by frying it, and then put it in a flannel bag. This was tied round the chest for pleurisy. She said her father always drank a tea made from wild mint and elderberry, to purify the liver and act as a cleanser.

9   *The Departed Village* by R.E. Moreau (OUP 1968, reprinted Readers' Union 1971, Newton Abbot), mentions a similar practice when nettle tea was imbibed 'to cool the blood' and 'ward off spots'.

10   This is the poignant inscription on a child's tombstone in St Andrew's churchyard only twenty yards from where I now sit typing. The carved headstone, like many in the churchyard carefully inscribed on 'imported' Cornish Delabole slate, is in memory of William Dawe, son of Henry and Elizabeth, who died on 2nd July 1821, aged two years.

   By wandering just a dozen paces either side of this pathetic little memorial, one can find many other resting places that bear witness to the terrible toll of infant mortality in the days before modern medicine.

   Nearby lie the remains of Rachel Foster, who passed away aged six years in June 1820, the daughter of James and Anne. Immediately below, on the same stone, is mention of another Rachel, of the same parents, who died at the age of twelve in 1842. Was this another little girl named by her grieving parents after the sister she never knew, only to be stricken down likewise in youth? What pain parents had to endure! Ironically the same tombstone shows that the bereaved parents not only outlived their children by many years, but survived for longer than most people expected in those days. Father James lived until he was sixty, and Mother Anne, who buried two daughters in that peaceful spot before either had reached their teens, soldiered on to eighty-one, being laid to rest beside her family in 1866.

Other graves beneath the giant yew tree and beside the rich green row of rhododendron shrubs that attract admiring visitors every year, make one wonder how anyone survived beyond school age.

'Sarah Lethbridge, died November 26th 1834, aged ten years . . . her brother Edwin died December 1834 aged four years and eleven months'.

What ailment robbed their parents of this brother and sister within a month of each other?

'Henry Harold, son of Robert and Elizabeth Camp, died Jan. 16th 1856 aged three years and four months . . .'

Another memorial nearby was erected to George Fox deceased aged 37 years, and also to his three children.

There is Joseph, aged four years who died in 1858, William, aged four who died in September 1864, and James, aged six, who also died in September 1864. Again two young brothers struck down by some killer disease in the same month . . . a family robbed of three young sons, all before school age, within a few years.

Jim Fox, (the lad who helped his father make the coffins) was leaning on the churchyard wall as my husband took a note of some of these gravestones.

"There's quite a few of us Foxes in here," he said, pointing to the last resting place of the three little brothers. He went on:

Terrible it was how young people got took, even in my young day. Thank God for modern medicines. I remember the days before they could do anything about tuberculosis. There used to be some sort of clinic up near the old aerodrome, where sufferers would come. You'd see them walking about. There was nothing to them, just a couple of legs and a frame on top. And when it came to burying them it was pathetic when they were in their coffins . . . just skin and bone.

Unless one tediously checks the dates on tombstones against other historical records, it is difficult to find out exactly what many youngsters died of. The fact that there are several buried, often from the same family, in a short period of time, points out to some kind of epidemic sweeping the area. The causes of death are rarely given.

But Jim reckoned there was at least one exception: Someone pointed out some gravestones to me once in Bere Alston churchyard which showed that the people had died from cholera. That was because no one was ever supposed to open up the grave of anyone who had died of cholera and you had to record the fact that they had died from it on the grave.

Back to Buckland Monachorum . . . and on the other side of the church, the pathetic rows of children's tombstones continue . . .

William Colwill, died April 1808 aged three years and six months
Betsy Colwill, died April 1803 aged one year
Susanna Colwill, died May 1808 aged one year and one month . . .

Chapter 5

11 *The Story of a School* 1675-1976 by R. Isherwood (available from St Andrew's School, Buckland Monachorum) describes a continuance of the village tradition of collecting eggs when 'in 1915 William Baker (the Headmaster) organised children's help for the sick and wounded soldiers, in which they collected 2,393 eggs in five months.'

12 *Horrabridge Village Book, ut supra,* also records this event: 'On September 10th 1915 the schoolchildren met at Horrabridge Railway Station at 9.30 a.m. to wave farewell to King George and Queen Mary who had been sleeping in their Royal Coach in the sidings for the previous two nights whilst during the day they had been visiting the Plymouth Hospitals to see the war victims. The children sang the National Anthem as their Majesties were leaving. School began at ten o'clock that morning.'

13 *Tavistock Goosie Fair* by Clive Gunnell (Bossiney Books), tells of a man called Norman Creber who, as a young boy, peeped through the shutters of his bedroom window at the rowdy events of the fair: 'It was always full of sailors. They would come up on the train from Plymouth and you've never seen such drinking and carrying on . . . On Goose Fair morning the first thing they did was take the pub doors off, unscrew the hinges and take the doors away—that way they could always get them out.'

Chapter 6

14 *The Gospel according to St Matthew* was published in a Devon dialect version in 1863 under the auspices of Prince Louis-Lucien Bonaparte, nephew of the great emperor.

15 *Industrial Archaeology of the Tamar Valley* by Frank Booker (David and Charles) devotes a chapter to the river steamers, and confirms that they were extremely comfortable: '. . . lockers throughout the length of the saloons were upholstered

115

with horsehair cushions covered in plush velvet, while mahogany tables ran down the centre. Room was provided for a piano, and there was apparatus for the preparation of tea and coffee. Even more revolutionary for the time was the toilet accommodation: separate lavatories were provided for men and women, it was proudly announced'.

Chapter 7

16 In *The Departed Village, ut supra*, the phrase 'weighed her thumb' is mentioned. This seems to be a common country suspicion.

17 The *Western Daily Mercury*, 28th July, 1913, recorded at the top of a page: A terrible tragedy . . . step sister shot by ex naval man . . . One of the most distressing Dartmoor tragedies on record will be enquired into this afternoon by a coroner's jury. It is embroidered in mystery and involves the sacrifice of two young lives, that of a pretty eighteen year old girl and her step brother who shot her with a double-barrelled breech-loading shotgun and then committed suicide . . . They are believed to have been on great terms of affection.

The newspaper, in a story filling a column, told how thirty-one year old William John Combes had come out of the navy only three months before the murder after completing twelve years service. He joined his relations in Buckland. His victim, Beatrice, had spent practically all her life at her moorland home and was 'beloved by everyone'. Neighbours spoke of her as 'the prettiest and most winsome girl in the village'.

18 Newspaper reports were able to fill in a few details that Joan, only ten at the time, has forgotten. Bill John Grepe (or Combes) had enjoyed a pint at the Drake Manor during lunchtime of Saturday the 26th, but was 'no worse for ale'. He walked about a mile to Didham Farm and borrowed a gun from the farmer, saying he wanted to shoot rabbits. Then he went down to see Mr Bere at the butcher's shop, because he wanted some cartridges. The butcher was out but his wife let him have half a dozen cartridges, and he said he would settle later. The *Mercury* journalist despatched to the village to report on the killings learned from the locals that 'Combe was unmarried and the girl also unattached, and for a long time they had shown a decided preference for one another's company.'

Even in those days the *Mercury* reporter was so struck by the charm of the village that as well as the gory details of the crime he devoted a few paragraphs to Buckland itself. Under a sub-heading 'An Old-World Spot', the paper went on: The village of Buckland Monachorum is a picturesque old-world spot two miles from Yelverton. It comprises little more than one street with masses of roses and

116

ivy geraniums clinging over the front of the houses. The church is rich in antiquity and has a brook rippling along its side.

On the morning of Wednesday, 30th July, the paper found space for a few more paragraphs about the poor brother and sister. They were squeezed in between items mentioning 'Johannesburg Riots . . . the black peril', Lord Gladstone, Lloyd George and Churchill. Under the heading 'The Dartmoor Crimes' it was noted that there was a large attendance of villagers at the funeral of the couple.

Chapter 8

19 *The story of a School, ut supra,* refers to the catalogue of educational supplies delivered from Plymouth for Mrs Baker's requirements, which is 'in its excessive simplicity a sharp contrast to the sophisticated equipment which flows into our schools today. Kate Baker's modest requirements comprised:

½ doz Midland Arithmetic Books, Standard IV

2 packets of Test cards

Foolscap paper

Box of Pens and Blotting Paper

½ doz dusters and 1 flannel

4 yards of calico, needles and buttons

1,000 attendance tickets

20 *Devon and Its People,* by Dr W.G. Hoskins (David and Charles) says that most people are surprised to know that before the Great War the single biggest occupation in Devon was domestic service—55,000 worked in it, 7,000 more than in farming, the recognised traditional industry of the county. He points out that for some time a great number of retired and well-to-do people had been coming to the West Country, attracted by the climate, beautiful scenery and the comparative cheapness of labour.

The Author has also referred to the following books and pamphlets, and with those listed above, recommends them for further reading.

Folklore and Customs of Rural England by Margaret Baker (David and Charles)

Folklore of Devon by S. Baring-Gould (Methuen & Co., MSS held by Plymouth City Library)

Songs of the West by S. Baring-Gould (Methuen & Co., MSS held by Plymouth City Library)

Cottage Life Book (The Countryman)

Guide to Dartmoor by William Crossing (David and Charles)

Dartmoor with a Difference by Lois Deacon (Toucan Press, Guernsey)

Daughter of Wyedean and Kernow—Notes from a West Country Childhood by Jessie Stoneham (Thornhill Press, Gloucester)

Lark Rise to Candleford by Flora Thompson (Penguin reprint)

Pamphlets:

Buckland Abbey Guide (Available from the Abbey and the National Trust)

St Andrew's Church Buckland Monachorum (available at the Church)

Lew Trenchard—the Manor House, the Church and Baring-Gould (S. Gordon Monk, 1961)

Lew Trenchard House and family history by present tenants (available at the house)